Life After Bristol City

SECOND SERIES

The Author

A former press officer and editor with two major national companies, Mark Leesdad has been following the fortunes (and misfortunes) of Bristol City since the early sixties. Days long before all-seater stadiums, zillion pound transfers and corporate hospitality. His hero was 'big' John Atyeo, described by latter-day hero Chris Garland as 'Mister Bristol City'.

An average winger (on a good day!) in local amateur soccer – he once scored against a Bristol Rovers youth team – he went on to enjoy managing the local village side that his sons Lee and Mark played in. These days he writes sports articles, including his weekly Memory Lane feature, in the *Sunday Independent*. He has also written the earlier volume one of *Life After Bristol City* and, together with James Ryan, assisted former City star Chris Garland with his autobiography, *A Life of Two Halves*.

He has been married to Jan for over thirty years, and the couple have two sons, two granddaughters and a grandson.

Life after Bristol City

SECOND SERIES

MARK LEESDAD

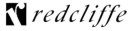 redcliffe

First published in 2009 by Redcliffe Press Ltd.,
81g Pembroke Road, Bristol BS8 3EA

www.redcliffepress.co.uk
info@redcliffepress.co.uk

© Mark Leesdad

ISBN   978-1-906593-08-7

British Library Cataloguing-in-Publication Data
A catalogue record for this book is available from the British Library

Design and typesetting by Steve Leary, steve@stevedesign.plus.com
Printed by HSW Print, Tonypandy

Contents

Acknowledgements 6
Introduction 7

Ian Baird	8	Andy Leaning	68
Darren Barnard	10	Gordon Low	70
Danny Bartley	12	John MacPhail	72
Peter Beadle	14	Jimmy Mann	74
Mickey Bell	16	Julian Marshall	76
Junior Bent	18	Hugh McIlmoyle	78
Terry Boyle	20	Micky Mellon	80
Russel Bromage	22	Steve Neville	82
Tony Butler	24	Kevin Nugent	84
Jack Connor	26	Gary Owers	86
Terry Connor	28	Glenn Pennyfather	88
Terry Cooper	30	Forbes Phillipson–Masters	90
Peter Cormack	32	Dickie Rooks	92
Alan Crawford	34	Joe Royle	94
Richard Dryden	36	Ray Savino	96
John Emmanuel	38	Martin Scott	98
Steve Galliers	40	Gerry Sharpe	100
Mark Gavin	42	George Showell	102
Mike Gibson	44	Ronnie Sinclair	104
Shaun Goater	46	Peter Spiring	106
Gerry Gow	48	Steve Stacey	108
Mick Harford	50	Mike Stowell	110
Nigel Hawkins	52	Alex Tait	112
Matt Hewlett	54	Bob Taylor	114
Chris Honor	56	Shaun Taylor	116
Glenn Humphries	58	Steve Thompson	118
Steve Johnson	60	Tony Thorpe	120
Joe Jordan	62	Derek Virgin	122
Martin Kuhl	64	Keith Waugh	124
John Kurila	66	Ken Wimshurst	126

Acknowledgements

Now look. You've taken the trouble to go out and purchase the book, so you can skip this bit if you want, it's not compulsory. But, if you do decide to read on, bear with me as I try not to go on too much about the numerous people I need to thank.

If you bought volume one of *Life After Bristol City*, you'll know that I thanked former bosses Christine Foster, Bill Edwardes and Richard Smith for all their help and guidance, as I turned to 'wordsmithing' as a career. And if you didn't buy volume one, then you'll be aware of my gratitude to them for the first time.

On the picture front I am once again indebted to photographer and good friend Phil McCheyne of Nailsea (I'm reliably informed he's in *Yellow Pages* and on the internet – www.philmccheynephoto.com). I have worked with Phil for a number of years now, been on hundreds of photo-shoots with him and rate him highly, which is why a number of the modern-day photographs in this book are his work. Also, my thanks to fellow author James Ryan (we worked on Chris Garland's autobiography – *A Life of Two Halves* – together) for helping me out with the proof reading.

As far as many of the playing days photographs are concerned, I must thank the various papers who allowed me to have them reproduced, another fellow author Mike Jay and, of course, many of the former players featured in this book, who rummaged through scrapbooks, cardboard boxes and suitcases (many of them stored in garages and attics) to find something that I could use. Ever conscious of copyright, I have not used any photographs carrying a copyright stamp without permission.

This book – and its predecessor – probably wouldn't have happened if *The Sunday Independent* and their sports supremo John Collings hadn't given me the go-ahead to write my weekly Memory Lane series, ultimately leading on to the idea being translated into book format. Thanks JC.

Special thanks for their faith in this project must also go my publishers, Bristol-based Redcliffe Press, experts in this field of work and renowned locally – a good combination.

Of course, all of these thank-yous would be completely irrelevant and meaningless if the players featured in these pages had not taken time out to answer a million questions about their lives, before, during and after their time with Bristol City. To all them, my grateful thanks. Without their help, cooperation and patience, this book wouldn't exist.

And finally, my thanks to YOU, the reader (hope there's more than one of you!) for buying this book. If you get as much pleasure reading it as I did meeting these Robins of yesteryear and writing their stories, then I'm a happy man.

Introduction

Don't blame me. If you're going to blame anyone, blame my brother Roy. 'Brilliant Bruv – when are you going to bring out a follow up?' It would have been a fair enough question, but he'd only had volume one of *Life After Bristol City* a week! Also, you're never quite sure when is a good time to bring out a 'follow up'. Since volume one came out, it's been a question of should I do another; will there be enough material; will people want to buy it?

As far as I'm concerned, the answer to the first two questions is 'yes'. Having met many of my former heroes of yesteryear and featured them in my weekly column in the *Sunday Independent* and in my first book, I have been lucky enough to have tracked down even more of them. To me, no look-back at City's former players would be complete without the likes of Terry Cooper, Joe Jordan, Sean Goater, Jack Connor, Jimmy Mann, Bob Taylor, Mike Gibson and oh so many more.

Will the public want to buy it? Well, unless you're just browsing in the bookshop or you've borrowed this from a friend, chances are you have bought it or some very wise person has bought it for you, in which case, Happy Birthday/Anniversary/Christmas.

For those of you who don't read the *Sunday Independent* or didn't buy a copy of *Life After Bristol City* (volume one) you'll need to know that this is a look at former Bristol City players, their time as professional footballers and their lives after soccer.

IAN BAIRD

A much travelled footballer during his playing days, Ian Baird started his career with Southampton in 1982. After just a handful of games for 'The Saints', plus loan spells at Cardiff and Newcastle, Ian moved to Leeds United, where he notched up over 100 appearances and scored 37 goals.

Just over two years after he joined Leeds, Portsmouth paid out £300,000 to bring Ian to Fratton Park, but the move was not a great success. When Leeds made a bid to re-sign their former striker, Ian was happy to return to Elland Road, playing another 91 games and scoring 21 more goals. A half-a-million pound transfer saw Ian move on to Middlesbrough, where he scored 19 times from his 63 appearances, before he headed to Scotland, in a £350,000 transfer to Hearts.

In July 1993, Ian moved back down south, signing for Bristol City. 'I'd played at Ashton Gate a few times and thought it was a good ground and also it wasn't a million miles from my roots at Southampton,' said Ian. 'Russell (Osman) sold the idea of signing for City to me, but it was an awkward time for him, making the step up from player to manager and trying to build his own team,' he added.

Not that Ian's stay at Ashton was all milk and honey. 'I'd been out injured with a hernia and made my come-back in a cup match against Stoke. I finished up with a collapsed lung and six broken ribs,' went on Ian. 'The club doctor didn't diagnose it and I drove back to Southampton in agony. I finished up in hospital and missed a couple of weeks, during which time the club had a good run, including that famous cup victory at Anfield.'

Desperate to reclaim his place in the side, Ian was pencilled in for a home match against Bolton. 'Then I got a rib infection, had to sit the game out and Russell ended up having to drive me home,' said Ian. Another spell in hospital followed, with Ian having a rib cut out and missing the rest of the season.

A losing run at the start of the new season spelt the end of Russell's time at City and Joe Jordan took over. 'I'd played for Joe at Hearts and rated him highly, but the rot had set in and he couldn't save the club from relegation,' pointed out Ian.

If injuries and then relegation weren't bad enough, Ian had a disastrous start to the following season. 'We were playing a friendly against Chelsea and a few of the fans started to get on my back. I reacted with a gesture and that spelt the end of my time with City.'

After City, where he'd played 57 times and scored 11 goals, came a season with Plymouth Argyle and two years at Brighton, before the injuries caught up with him and he retired, having made around 450 Football League appearances. The next stop was Asia and during his time in Hong Kong, Ian took charge of a side from their top division and also managed the national side.

On returning to the UK, Ian was a football agent for a while and also ran Southampton's Youth Academy. These days he's a director for a car sales and vehicle leasing business. And Ian's still very much involved in the soccer scene, managing non-league side Eastleigh.

Married to Christina, Ian has two daughters, one son and a grandson.

Ian during his playing days at Argyle.
(photo: *Sunday Independent*)

Company director and football manager, Ian Baird
today.

DARREN BARNARD

Probably the only thing predictable about a career in football is its unpredictability. Take former City favourite Darren Barnard. A talented natural left-sided player, he was established at Bristol City, had just signed a new three-year contract and was about to buy a house in the area. Then he gets transferred.

'I'd had two seasons with City and it was all going well,' said Darren. 'Originally I was commuting from Surrey and then I rented a house in Bradley Stoke. After signing the new deal we were on the verge of buying our own place, when Barnsley came in for me.'

Born in Germany ('Dad was in the forces'), Darren was turned down as an apprentice by Spurs. So he signed for non-league Wokingham Town and at 16 was a first team regular. Showing a maturity way beyond his years, he weighed in with 14 goals, many of them free kicks and penalties.

It was during his one season at Wokingham that Darren came under the scrutiny of the scouts. And so he ended up signing for Chelsea and a delighted Wokingham were £100,000 richer.

After a two-year wait, Darren finally made his league debut. He was to make 29 senior appearances, (scoring twice) and was a first-half substitute in the side that beat Luton Town in the '94 FA Cup semi-final. But, when it came to the final, Darren wasn't even on the bench for a game that Chelsea lost four-nil to an Eric Cantona-inspired Man United.

'I felt I stagnated a bit at Chelsea,' said Darren. 'I did have a month's loan at Reading and would have stayed longer, but the manager left and it fell through.'

But, in early October '95, City paid Chelsea £750,000 to bring Darren to Ashton Gate. 'Joe Jordan was the manager and he scared the living daylights out of me – especially when he took his teeth out! I'd never even played at Bristol before, it was all new to me,' said Darren. 'Originally I was in midfield, but then Joe moved me to left back.'

During his time at City, Darren struck up a good partnership down the left flank with Brian Tinnion. 'We played well together and always instinctively knew where the other would be.'

The signing of Mickey Bell in the summer of '97 promised great things down the left flank. But any such dreams were dashed before they had started, as a £750,000 cheque from Premier League new boys Barnsley saw Darren depart for Oakwell, after 94 City appearances and 17 goals.

'As a footballer you always want to play against the best and the chance to do so in the Premiership was too good to turn down,' admitted Darren.

Barnsley's big adventure in the top division was to last just one season. 'It would have been a fantastic achievement just to stay up, but it wasn't to be,' said Darren, who had five years at Oakwell, made over 200 appearances and scored 28 goals. He also won 24 caps for Wales.

After Barnsley, Darren had two seasons with Grimsby Town, before dropping down to the Conference with Aldershot. He made some 127 appearances for 'The Shots', many as skipper, before departing for a new challenge with Counties League side Camberley Town, where he has the treble role of player, coach and director of football.

Married to Michaela, the couple live in Surrey with their three young sons, Daniel, Joshua and Luke.

Darren in league action.
(photo: *Grimsby Telegraph*)

Darren pictured on a day out with son Joshua.

DANNY BARTLEY

When you're a young footballer, not long married and settled in your home, the last thing you really want to hear is that your club has accepted an offer for you and you could be on your way, putting down new roots in a strange area. But such is the lot of many a professional footballer. And so it was with City outside-left Danny Bartley.

'The club rang to say that they'd agreed a fee with Swansea to sign me and team mate Dave Bruton,' recalled Danny. 'I wasn't over keen, but when I met their manager, Harry Gregg, and looked round the area, I took to the place immediately.'

And so began a new chapter for Danny, who took to Swansea like the proverbial duck takes to Welsh water.

Long before the question of whether or not to 'cross the bridge' came along, a young Danny started his career with Bristol City as an apprentice in 1964. 'Fred Ford was the boss and he was an outstanding manager,' said Danny. 'He gave me my full debut at seventeen and I made a couple of goals in a home win over Carlisle, which was a good start.'

Danny was also to enjoy success with the England Youth team, winning five caps and playing alongside the likes of Frank Lampard (senior), Alec Lindsay and Norman Piper.

Between 1966 and 1973, Danny was to make over 100 senior appearances for The Robins. One of the games that stood out for him was John Atyeo's last game, with 'Big John' needing two goals to reach the magical 350 mark. 'We played Ipswich in the final match of the season. John was a legend at the club and he managed to grab the two goals that gave him the three hundred and fifty, one of them coming when he got the faintest of touches to my in-swinging corner,' reminisced Danny. But was Danny's corner actually over the line before John got that touch? 'Many people behind the goal say it was, but no one, me included, would want to deny John his last moment of glory.'

It was at the start of the 73/74 season that Danny got the call about a possible transfer to Wales. 'Obviously it was a wrench, having to up sticks and so on, but it turned out to be the best move I ever made,' he admitted.

Danny's first season at The Vetch saw the team battling at the wrong end of the Fourth Division table. But the following year they improved, the start of what was to become part of a golden age in Swansea's history, with successive promotions during the John Toshack revolution.

Although Danny was to enjoy Swansea's halcyon days, it was mainly as a full back, rather than winger, that he featured. 'We had an injury crisis and the boss said he wanted me to play left back,' revealed Danny. 'I'd never played there before, but the manager insisted and that was that.'

But after seven years and over 200 games for 'The Swans', Danny moved on, spending three years with Hereford United, before dropping into non-league football. For the past 22 years, he has been the local manager for a finance company.

Married to childhood sweetheart Mary, the couple live in Dunvant in South Wales. They have a son, Kevin, who was on Cardiff's books at one time and daughter Nicola, who is a beautician.

Danny in his playing days.

Danny Bartley on a recent return trip to
Ashton Gate.

PETER BEADLE

To play for both Bristol clubs is a pretty big challenge to most players. If, for example, you leave Rovers to join City, your old Rovers fans think you're a traitor, while many City fans will still think of you as 'the enemy'. Like a number of players who have made the trip 'across town', Peter Beadle found the transition quite daunting to start with. 'I think I managed to win over most of the City fans, but there will always be those who couldn't forgive me for playing for Rovers,' said Peter.

An old-fashioned centre forward, Peter started out on soccer's rocky road at Gillingham. His whole-hearted displays soon attracted the attention of scouts from the higher divisions and, in 1992, after 67 league appearances and 14 goals for 'The Gills', a dream move materialized, when Terry Venables signed him for Tottenham Hotspur. Unfortunately for Peter, Venables left to be replaced by Ossie Ardilles and it was time for Peter to start packing, leaving Spurs without a senior league appearance to his name. 'I guess one of them rated me and the other didn't,' he summed up.

After temporary stops at Bournemouth and Southend, Peter was off to Elton John's Watford, where he enjoyed moderate success, before he headed to the South West in November '95 to don the blue-and-white quarters of Bristol Rovers. Here he came into his own and in two-and-a-half years with 'The Gas' scored 43 goals.

After over a century of Rovers appearances, Peter left for short spells with Port Vale and Notts County, before returning to Bristol in October '99 to try his luck with City. 'There were plenty of people who told me it wouldn't work out at City, given my Rovers connection and the fact that I'd scored against them. But I've never shirked a challenge and I signed for them, determined to give it my best shot.'

Peter was to spend the best part of four years at Ashton Gate, during which time he won over most of the sceptics. He made 82 league appearances and scored 14 goals, many of them vital match winners. In his last season he experienced the heartbreak of losing out in the Play Offs, but had the consolation of being in the squad when they won the LDV Vans Trophy at Cardiff's Millenium Stadium.

Released by City in 2003, Peter's next move was to prove a disaster. Given a short-term contract by Brentford, he was sent off 10 minutes into his debut and was then on the injured list following a training ground mishap. A month later he moved on to (then) non-league Barnet, before returning to this neck of the woods to play non league football with Team Bath and later Clevedon Town, where he was also commercial manager. He stepped up to the manager's chair at Taunton Town and in October 2005 took over the hot seat at Conference South club Newport County.

Under Beadle, County twice missed out on the Conference South play offs and appeared twice in the FAW Premier Cup Final, winning it in 2008. They also enjoyed some decent runs in the FA Cup. Despite this, County's priority was to get promotion and failure to do so saw a parting of the ways in April 2008.

Peter as a Bristol City player.

Older but wiser, Peter Beadle today.

MICKEY BELL

'Never a dull moment,' was how Mickey Bell described his time at Ashton Gate. And there certainly weren't many dull moments for him during those eight seasons. Promotion in his first season, relegation and a broken leg in his second and a seemingly never ending succession of managers.

'I was signed by John Ward and, after him there was Benny Lennartson, Tony Pulis, Dave Burnside, Leroy Rosenior, Tony Fawthrop, Danny Wilson and Brian Tinnion,' recalled Mickey.

A member of the Newcastle Boys team, Geordie-born Mickey was spotted by a scout for Northampton Town, who signed him on as an apprentice. 'In those days I played on the left of midfield,' pointed out Mickey, who went on to complete over 150 league appearances in the old Third and Fourth Divisions for 'The Cobblers', scoring 10 goals.

In October '94, League newcomers Wycombe Wanderers moved in to sign Mickey. 'One of the reasons I'd signed for them was the manager – Martin O'Neill. A fantastic motivator,' he said.

It was during his time at Wycombe that Mickey was switched to left back and he went on to play well over a century of league games for 'The Chairboys'. But, to the dismay of management and fans alike, Mickey, who had just won the Player of the Year award, moved on in the summer of '97, signing for newly-promoted City for £150,000.

Mickey's first season at Ashton Gate couldn't have gone any better. Virtually an ever present, Mickey and his team mates enjoyed the thrill of promotion, with Mickey not only a star defender, but goalscorer as well, with a haul of 10 goals to his credit. 'I think six or seven of those came from the penalty spot,' he pointed out.

But, having enjoyed a perfect first season, Mickey's second year was the complete opposite. 'I ended up on the injured list with a broken leg, John Ward left and the side was relegated – a terrible season.'

Despite relegation and the continuing chopping and changing of managers, Mickey still went on to complete nearly 350 games for City, scoring 39 times. 'There were some excellent players at the club during my time there. Shaun Taylor – a giant of a player; Louis Carey – young but awesome; Shaun Goater, who was scoring goals for fun and 'Tins' (Brian Tinnion) who I had a great understanding with down the left.'

But, in 2004, City released Mickey. 'It was a wrench to leave. I had hoped to finish my career with City, but that's football,' he said philosophically. Given a choice of Port Vale or Cheltenham Town, Mickey plumped for the Potteries side, a decision he was to regret.

'At the start it was fine, then the club started selling their best players and, on top of that, my wife Jane didn't really want to move. In fairness, the club were very good and helped me get fixed up with Cheltenham.'

Reunited with former City boss John Ward, Mickey helped his new club to promotion from League Two, coming on as a sub in the Play Off final against Grimsby at Wembley, but time was catching up on him. 'I kept getting injured, mainly Achilles problems, and ended up having an operation. The surgeon told me my full time playing days were over.'

Since leaving full time football, Mickey has had spells with Weston-super-Mare and Team Bath. He lives in Nailsea with wife Jane, daughters Penny and Megan and son Sam.

Editor Mark Leesdad joins Mickey, Peter
Beadle and 'Robbie Robin' (alias City old
boy Gerry Sweeney) for a Christmas training
session at Ashton Gate during Mickey's
playing days at City.

Mickey Bell today.

JUNIOR BENT

It was a pretty fair bet that if Junior Bent was playing for City at Ashton Gate during the nineties, you were looking at a 'banker home'. So, it's quite appropriate that, since leaving professional football, Junior has been very much involved in the banking business.

Born in Huddersfield, the diminutive outside right joined his home town club as a trainee. In the late eighties he made some 40 senior league appearances for 'The Terriers', plus around a dozen games on loan for Burnley, before coming to Bristol City.

'I signed on deadline day 1990, with the club on the verge of promotion from the old Third Division,' recalled Junior. City boss Joe Jordan paid Huddersfield £30,000 for Junior, a wise investment, given that he would become a firm favourite. He made the first of over 200 appearances in a City shirt as a sub in the last home game of that promotion season, a 4-nil victory over Walsall.

'There was a good management team at the club, led by Joe, who could always get the best out of his players. He was red hot on fitness and also a very honest and fair manager,' said Junior.

One of the highlights of Junior's seven years at City came in the 93/94 season, when the club got through to the last 16 of the FA Cup, defeating mighty Liverpool on their own ground, after drawing at Ashton Gate. Junior turned in one of his best performances in a City shirt, giving Scottish international Steve Nichol a torrid time. 'The City win at Anfield – not a game you forget in a hurry,' said Junior with a smile.

When it came to away games, Junior usually roomed with full back Andy Llewellyn. 'It was all part of Joe's strategy,' said Junior. 'He would look to pair up players that would be working closest together during the game. Obviously I would be most involved during the match with our right back, so Louie and I would room together.'

During his time at City, Junior played under Jordan (twice), Jimmy Lumsden, Denis Smith, Russell Osman and John Ward. He had a loan spell at Stoke, before enjoying his most consistent run in the side during the 94/95 and 95/96 seasons, when he was virtually an ever present. He also had a loan spell with Shrewsbury, before calling time on his stay at Bristol in 1997, after 221 games and 23 goals for the club.

'I was a bit out of favour at the time and had the chance to move back nearer my roots with Blackpool,' explained Junior. ' I remember going back to City with Blackpool and wondering what sort of reception I'd get. I needn't have worried – the City fans had always been very good to me and I got a standing ovation, which meant a lot.'

A change of manager spelt the end of Junior's time with 'The Seasiders' and, although offered the chance of a contract with Plymouth Argyle, he decided to call it a day.

After successfully completing the necessary courses, Junior worked for HSBC as a customer advisor, before moving on to be a branch manager. Two-and-a-half years later, he became a freelance mortgage consultant, before returning to banking as a branch manager for Barclays. He has since taken up the position of business relationship manager with the Royal Bank of Scotland.

Married to Beverley, the couple have two young sons, Jordan and Cory.

Junior during his City days.

Still looking pretty fit, Junior Bent today.

TERRY BOYLE

When Welsh international Terry Boyle swapped the bright lights of London for Bristol in 1981, he knew he was joining a club that was on a bit of a slide. Two successive relegation seasons had seen them drop from the (old) First Division into the Third. He could have been forgiven for thinking that it couldn't get any worse.

'It soon became evident that not only was the club struggling on the pitch, but financially as well,' said Terry, now a football development officer with the Welsh FA.

Terry came to Bristol, leaving top-flight club Crystal Palace as part of the deal that saw City striker Kevin Mabbutt move in the opposite direction. Although born in Ammanford, Terry started life as a young professional with Spurs in 1975. He moved on to Crystal Palace in 1978, staying at Selhurst Park for some three years and making over 30 senior appearances, but it should have been more, but for injuries. He also had a short loan spell with Wimbledon.

Although Kevin Mabbutt was highly thought of at Ashton Gate, City manager Bob Houghton decided to let him go to Palace, with Terry coming to City. This would be the chance to shore up the team's leaky defence, while at the same time bringing much needed funds into the club – Palace also parting with £100,000 as part of the deal.

'There were some good players at City, a great bunch of lads, despite the club's problems,' said Terry, who made his debut in a goalless draw with Chesterfield.

By the following January, the well documented financial crash and the redundancy offer to the 'Ashton Gate Eight' brought the club's affairs to a head. 'That was a terrible period,' commented Terry. 'I played in what could have been Bristol City's last ever game, at Newport County. It was a very worrying time.'

History shows that, thanks to the sacrifice of the eight players involved, Bristol City did survive. After such an 'on the brink of disaster' situation, relegation to the league's bottom flight was of little consequence in comparison to what could have happened.

Relishing his role as captain, Terry and his team mates began life in the Fourth Division under the managership of Terry Cooper – messrs Houghton and Hodgson having departed for financially healthier pastures. It was during the early part of the new (82/83) season that Terry scored his two Bristol City goals – both against Swindon in the old Milk Cup competition. But with City third from bottom of the Fourth, a chance to return to the 'land of his fathers' in early November was taken by Terry, as he signed for Third Division Newport County.

Terry was to play over 150 games for Newport, before moving just down the road to Cardiff City, where he played a similar number of games, before completing a hat trick of Welsh moves with a season at Swansea, where he wound up his league playing days. Altogether, he played in over 700 league and cup games (including 46 appearances for City) during his career. He has also represented his country at all levels.

After playing in the Welsh non-league circuit, Terry became assistant manager to Welshpool Town in the Welsh Premier League.

Living just outside Bangor, Terry is employed by the FA of Wales Trust as development officer for Gwynedd, helping to establish youth soccer throughout Wales.

Terry in his City days.

Taking a training session at Welshpool.
(photo: Graham Lewis)

RUSSEL BROMAGE

Life has been full of aches and 'panes' for Russel Bromage. For, in addition to bearing the scars of being a professional footballer, former City full back Russel Bromage has been a window cleaner for the past 13 years – hence the panes!

Born in The Potteries, Russel joined his local side Port Vale as an apprentice, going on to make his debut as a substitute at the age of 16. Predominantly a left back, he went on to play 400 games for 'The Valiants' and became a firm favourite with the home fans, winning the Player of the Year award in 1981.

In the summer of 1987, City manager Terry Cooper agreed a fee of around £25,000 to bring Russel to Ashton Gate. 'I'd played against City a few times over the years and was always impressed with the club and the set up there, although I don't think I ever lost playing against them at Ashton Gate,' he recalled.

The first shock for Russel was discovering just how big Bristol is. 'When you only know a place from travelling for football, you don't realise just how large an area is, but I loved it there and made a lot of friends in the area,' he said.

'Derby games against Rovers were always a bit special, always fiercely contested tight matches, though I don't think I was ever on the winning side against them,' he admitted.

Russel went on to notch over 50 games for The Robins, a figure that would have been greater, but for an Achilles problem that kept him on the sidelines for the best part of a year. Full backs aren't supposed to be high scorers, and Russel got just the one goal in a City shirt. 'That was a right-foot drive against Preston at Ashton Gate. It was from all of five yards and I think the pace of it deceived their keeper as it trickled past him! I could be deadly from close in!'

With Russel still struggling for full fitness and his contract up in 1990, he was surprised to get an offer to join Brighton, following his release from City. 'I told them straight about my injuries, but got through the medical and they gave me a two-year contract,' he recalled.

But Russel's niggling injury problems came back with a vengeance, restricting him to just a few appearances with 'The Seagulls'. 'I spent a lot of time working with the club's youngsters and the local school of excellence, but called it a day in 1992,' he said. After football Russel literally took steps to forge a new career – cleaning windows.

But he's not completely severed his ties with the world of soccer. He is also assistant manager for Sussex County League side Whitehawk.

Married to Candy, the couple have two young sons and live in beautiful Shoreham in West Sussex.

'I made a lot of friends during my time in Bristol and have some fond memories of my time there. There were some very good players and some great characters at the club,' said Russel. 'Andy Llewellyn, Steve Galliers, Rob Newman, David Moyes and a team mate called Steve McClaren. I wonder whatever happened to him!'

Russel during his time at City.

A more recent photo of Russel Bromage.
(photo: *The Argus*, Brighton)

TONY BUTLER

Central defender Tony Butler clocked up nearly 500 Football League games, been involved in transfers totalling over half a million pounds and twice suffered the agony of Play Off defeat while wearing the red and white of Bristol City.

Spotted by Gillingham as a youngster, Tony went to the Kent club for trials and earned himself a YTS contract. 'I actually made my senior debut while on the youth scheme,' said Tony, who went on to play over 150 games for 'The Gills'. But, despite winning promotion from the old Third Division at the end of the 95/96 season, Tony wanted away. 'I just fancied a new challenge,' he explained. 'I was on the verge of signing for Preston, when their local rivals Blackpool, managed by Gary Megson, came in for me and I joined them.'

A fee of £250,000 was set by a tribunal and Tony went on to have one of the most enjoyable spells of his career. 'I had three years there and loved it,' said Tony. But, in March '99, on the eve of the transfer deadline, Tony was on his way to Port Vale, then playing in the First Division (now The Championship). It wasn't the best of times for Tony, with injuries restricting him to just a couple of dozen games. But, almost a year to the day, he was involved in another deadline-day deal, linking up again with former Blackpool boss Megson at West Brom.

Tony made his debut for 'The Baggies' two days later – a 2-1 defeat at Manchester City – and the following season was virtually an ever present, as the side reached the First Division (Championship) Play Offs. It was to be the first of a hat trick of Play Off heartaches, as Bolton pipped them for top flight status. They went one better the following season, enjoying Play Off success, but the following summer Tony was on his way to Ashton Gate.

'Danny Wilson brought me to City and I had three years with the club,' continued Tony. 'I was impressed with the management team that they had in place and also with some of the exciting youngsters they had coming through.'

With Tony one of the first names on the team sheet, it was a case of 'so near yet so far' as City lost out to Cardiff in the Play Off semis in his first season and were then defeated by Brighton in the final the following year, which signalled the end of Wilson's time in charge. 'We just kept falling at the final fence and although we won the LDV Vans Trophy in 2003, promotion was always the priority.'

With Wilson gone and Brian Tinnion in the manager's chair, City finished a disappointing seventh at the end of that season, which also saw Tony leave City after nearly 100 games. 'It was all very amicable,' said Tony. 'I was still living in Cheshire and stopping over at Peter Beadle's place a couple of days a week, so when I had the chance of a move nearer the family home I jumped at it.'

After winding up his league career with 'The Seasiders', Tony dropped into non-league football, playing for Forest Green, Newport County and Hinckley United. He currently plays for Blue Square Conference side Alfreton Town.

Away from football, Tony, who holds an HGV2 licence, works for a local building firm. He lives in Nantwich with wife Nicola and young children James and Olivia.

Tony in action for City.

Tony Butler today.

JACK CONNOR

Back in the sixties, City's regular centre half was a certain Jack Connor. Brought down from Huddersfield by manager Fred Ford, he could not only take care of the centre of City's defence, but could also get forward and pop the odd goal in. The only trouble was, he also occasionally 'popped one in' at the wrong end, past his own keeper! 'I think I'm probably a couple of goals up in the 'goals for' column!' laughed Jack, when reminded of this fact.

Born in Cumberland, Jack joined Huddersfield Town as a teenager and clearly remembers making his league debut. 'It was against Manchester United and I was marking the legendary Duncan Edwards – a nice easy one to start with!'

In October 1960 Jack began his long association with Bristol City, moving to the South West in straight swop deal for Johnny McCann. It was to prove to be a shrewd piece of business. 'I had been at Huddersfield eight or nine seasons and played close on a hundred games for them when City came in for me,' recalled Jack. 'Initially I wasn't that keen on the move, but I travelled to Bristol to discuss the transfer with Fred Ford and he 'sold' the club to me. I took to him straightaway and it turned out to be a really good move.'

Jack went on to forge a good central defensive partnership with his friend and old Huddersfield team mate Gordon Low, who joined him at City five months later. 'There were some very good players at the club,' recalled Jack. 'Tommy Casey, who was arguably the most enthusiastic player I ever met: full back Mike Thresher, a superb defender and wingers Lou Peters and Jantzen Derrick. And, of course, 'Big John' (Atyeo), who was different class.'

Fred Ford was building a strong team capable of going up from the (old) Third Division, and in 1965, the side, with Jack virtually an ever present, clinched promotion by winning their last game of the season. Over 28,000 fans crammed into Ashton Gate to see them beat an Oldham Athletic side that included Jack's predecessor, Alan Williams. 'A wonderful occasion,' said Jack, with a smile that was never far from his lips throughout his career.

Adapting to life at the higher level, Jack went on to clock up over 400 games for The Robins, before stepping down at 35 to be replaced by Dickie Rooks. For a while he took on a coaching position at Ashton Gate and later had a similar role at Everton, before leaving the game.

'I was a sales rep for fifteen years, working for a company that supplied cargo control equipment and also had a spell running a sports and social club in Bootle,' revealed Jack.

Jack lives in Formby with his wife Chris. 'It's a lovely part of the world, about eight miles from Southport and fifteen from Liverpool,' said Jack. And he still follows the game. 'It's totally different now of course. In my day we didn't play four-four-two, we played two-three-five(!), but in so many other ways I do think it's better,' he said. 'The players are much fitter and the stadiums are a million miles away from what they used to be like.'

Jack in his City days.

Jack Connor today.

TERRY CONNOR

Leeds born and bred, Terry Connor joined his local club as a schoolboy. Progress-ing through the youth ranks, he signed as a full-time professional under Jimmy Adamson, with Dave Merrington (another to have worn City's red and white) as his number two.

'It was a great privilege to sign for Leeds United,' said Terry. 'The club had achieved so much and it's sad to see the way they have gone down the Divisions over the last few years.'

Between 1979 and 1983, Terry was to make over 100 appearances for the Elland Road club, scoring 22 goals. He left in March 1983, moving to Brighton in a deal worth £500,000 that saw Andy Ritchie moving in the opposite direction. 'By that time Leeds had already dropped down to the old Second Division, while Brighton were in the First and on their way to an FA Cup Final with Man United,' pointed out Terry.

Because Terry had been cup-tied playing for Leeds, he didn't get to line up for Brighton in the two cup final matches (the game going to a replay) and, in addition to losing, the club was relegated. But Terry enjoyed his stay on the South Coast. 'It was a smashing part of the world and I loved my four years there,' he said. It was while Terry was at Brighton that he was selected for international honours with the England under-21s.

After around 200 games for 'The Seagulls', Terry moved on to Portsmouth, but his time at Fratton Park was beset by injury. 'I had trouble with my hips and ligaments and only made around fifty appearances for them in my three years there,' revealed Terry.

Former Leeds colleague Terry Yorath took Terry to Swansea in the summer of 1990. 'That was good because Swansea had got into Europe after winning the Welsh Cup and I got to play in far-off places like Monaco,' he recalled.

It was in September '91 that Terry came to Ashton Gate. 'Jimmy Lumsden, an excellent coach, was the man who signed me and later I played under Denis Smith,' said Terry.

'There were some very good players there – Bob Taylor, Martin Scott, Gary Shelton and Keith Welch spring to mind.'

But Terry was still struggling for full fitness and after 16 league appearances, he went back to Swansea. 'I then had a spell in non-league with Yeovil, but that proved to be too much – my knee simply wasn't up to it,' he admitted.

A spell with Swindon helping to run their centre of excellence followed, before he linked up with John Ward at Rovers, taking on the role of community officer. When Ward moved across town to City in 1997, Terry followed as coach, helping to develop promising youngsters such as Matt Hewlett, Louis Carey and Tommy Doherty.

Under John Ward, City won promotion to football's second tier, but the following season City started badly and Ward was axed. 'John moved on to work for Colin Lee as his assistant at Wolves and I rejoined him at Molineux and have been here ever since,' summed up the man who played nearly 400 senior games, scored over 100 goals and is assistant manager to Mick McCarthy at Molineux.

Married to Jan, the couple live in Sutton Coldfield and have three children – Hayley, a dentistry student at Bristol University and twins Nicole and Louis, who are both still at school.

Terry in his City days.

Terry Connor, now assistant manager at Wolves.

TERRY COOPER

What can you write about Terry Cooper that hasn't already been written? This is a man who has played 20 times for England, made around 400 senior games for one of the country's leading clubs, won practically every trophy in football and has played for and managed both Bristol clubs.

Yorkshire-born Terry was converted from outside left to left back by the legendary Don Revie. He never looked back, as Leeds United dominated the top flight of English football for years. He scored the winning goal in the 1968 League Cup Final, was a member of the title winning side of 1969 and only missed the 1972 Cup Final through injury. And, of course, there was that 'little matter' of playing for England in the 1970 World Cup Finals.

'Mexico was a fantastic experience, although I must admit I felt a bit jaded, having played over seventy games for Leeds that season,' confessed Terry.

In March 1975, Terry left Leeds, joining his old team mate Jack Charlton, at Middlesbrough. After over 100 games there, Terry signed for Bristol City in a £20,000 transfer in 1978. 'Alan Dicks signed me and it was great to link up again with Norman (Hunter), although I had a few injury problems and didn't really do myself justice there first time around,' he admitted.

After just a handful of games for City, Terry moved across town to Rovers, taking on the role of player manager. He was to play 59 times for 'The Pirates', before a parting of the ways in November '81 saw him leave, joining another old team mate, Billy Bremner, at Doncaster Rovers.

Less than a year later, Terry was heading back to Ashton Gate, where City had sunk to the bottom division, following the financial disaster that had hit the club earlier in the year. 'When I came back to City, the only way was up,' said Terry. 'I had to rebuild on a shoe string, but there were some good youngsters there and an excellent chairman in Des Williams.'

Terry was certainly the man to answer City's prayers and, after stabilizing the sinking ship, he produced a promotion-winning side which also went on to win the Freight Rover Trophy at Wembley. But nothing lasts for ever and after six years (and another 60 appearances as a player) Terry moved on. He had three good years managing Exeter City, before getting the call to manage Birmingham City.

'Birmingham are a huge club and managing them was a great experience, especially winning promotion in my first season,' said Terry. 'The only trouble was there was a fair bit of 'boardroom politics' in play.'

After Terry left Birmingham, he was tempted back to troubled Exeter. 'With hindsight that was a mistake on my part,' he admitted. 'The club went bust and the whole thing became a nightmare.'

After six months managing in impossible circumstances, Terry had had enough. 'We moved to Tenerife and I intended to retire,' he explained. 'Then, after a year out of football, I got a call asking me to join the scouting team at Southampton,' said Terry, who spent eight years as 'The Saints' European scout.

Married to Rosemary, the couple still live in Tenerife. And although Terry has now stepped down from the hustle and bustle of soccer life, the name Cooper continues to make the back page headlines, thanks to son Mark, who is manager of FA Cup giant-killers, Conference side Kettering Town.

Terry in his playing days.

A more recent photograph of Terry.

PETER CORMACK

Everyone knows the legend that is Bill Shankly, but most people don't know that Bill was one of five brothers. And one of his them, Bob, was also a football manager. Former Scottish international Peter Cormack played for both of them.

'I started off on the Hearts ground staff, but later signed professional forms for Hibs, managed by Bob Shankly,' revealed Peter.

It was during his time at Hibs that Peter won the first of nine Scottish caps, a one-all draw at Hampden, against the mighty Brazil. 'A special moment for me,' recalled Peter. 'Brazil were a great side and I still have Gerson's shirt from that game.'

Peter played 182 games for Hibs, scoring 75 goals and was their top scorer for two successive seasons. In March 1970, an £80,000 cheque took Peter to Nottingham Forest. But, with relegation from the top flight at the end of the 71/72 season a move, after 86 appearances and 20 goals, was always likely.

'Spurs were looking to sign me, but when Bill Shankly came in for me, I was more than happy to go to Anfield,' said Peter.

To write about what Peter achieved during his four years at Liverpool would take up a book of its own. So, in brief, Peter went on to become a key member of the team that completed a League and UEFA Cup double and won the FA Cup. There were also two Charity Shield finals.

All in all, Peter made 178 appearances for the club. But an injury in October '76 forced him to miss the rest of the season, which saw the side emulate their success of 1973, when they once again made it a League and UEFA Cup double. Still struggling for full fitness, Peter found his way into the side blocked by the emergence of Ray Kennedy as a midfielder.

The chance to play First Division football again came when Bristol City, anxious to preserve their top flight status, persuaded him to swop Anfield for Ashton. 'City had a good ground, great support and, with so many Scots already on the books, it was home from home for me,' said Peter. 'Alan Dicks took a gamble on my fitness and it paid off.'

Peter was to spend over three years with City, making 65 appearances and scoring 10 times. And it was not the end of his collection of winners' medals either. Although the Anglo-Scottish Cup isn't perhaps in the same league as the FA or UEFA Cup, he scored the goal that saw City win the trophy in 1977.

In February 1980, with the club fighting a losing battle against relegation, Peter was released, moving back to Hibs. 'I didn't have much of a say about staying,' he admitted. 'The club was having financial problems and with so many good players gone, they were always going to struggle. Having said that, I enjoyed my time there.'

After Hibs, Peter managed Partick Thistle, coached in Cyprus, took charge of the Botswana national team, was assistant manager back at Hibs and had an astonishing 'ten days only' spell as manager of Cowdenbeath, walking away after internal problems, without taking charge of the team for a single game. His last management post was at Morton.

Now in his early sixties, Peter lives with wife Marion in Edinburgh and can often be found on the after-dinner circuit, regaling fans with his footballing stories and anecdotes.

Peter in action for City.

Plenty of interesting and amusing stories from
Peter the after-dinner speaker.

ALAN CRAWFORD

L ife has gone full cycle for former City winger Alan Crawford. Born in Rotherham, he signed schoolboy forms for his local club, served his apprenticeship and
went on to become a firm favourite there, totting up over 250 senior appearances and
consistently finding the back of the net. Now, more than 40 years on, he's back where
it all started.

On 'The Millers' books at the age of 13, Alan became a regular in the Rotherham
first team in the 73/74 season, having made his senior debut at the age of 17. He
went on to appear in 168 consecutive games and was a key member of the side that
won promotion to the Third Division in 1975. The following season he found the net
31 times, a staggering tally for a left winger. 'I had the advantage of being the side's
penalty taker and that season we had thirteen pens, which is a lot.'

Despite enjoying cult status at the club, Alan parted company with them in 1979,
linking up with Chesterfield, where he enjoyed three seasons and was a member of
the team that won the Anglo-Scottish Cup and twice just missed promotion.

In August 1982, with Bristol City still recovering from the financial disaster of the
previous season, Alan joined a City side being rebuilt by Terry Cooper. 'It was very
much a transitional time for the club, and I was proud to be part of it,' said Alan. 'I was
impressed by Terry [Cooper], top man as far as I am concerned.'

Alan's first year at Ashton Gate was one of stabilisation for the club. At one time they
were bottom of the Fourth Division, before finishing in mid-table. Alan was virtually
an ever present, scoring seven goals. 'I might have got more, but the club already had
a regular penalty taker in Tom Ritchie,' he pointed out.

The following season saw City rise from the ashes and win promotion. It was
during that year that Alan scored his one and only hat trick, against Torquay United.
'My old Chesterfield team mate John Turner was in goal for them,' he recalled with
a smile.

In the summer of 1985, with 105 senior appearances and 28 goals for City, Alan left
for Exeter City. Ironically, he came back to Ashton Gate to play City in an FA Cup
game and scored one of his side's goals in a 2-1 win.

A season at Bath City was next on the agenda and again Alan faced his old City
team mates in the FA Cup, although this time he wasn't able to put one over on his
old club. Drawn to play at home, Bath switched the game to Ashton Gate and fought
out a creditable one-all draw, before losing the replay 3-0.

'After that I had a spell managing Western League side Bristol Manor Farm. It was
good experience and, as I was still living in Nailsea, suited me perfectly.' And when
City offered Alan a role on the coaching staff, he didn't need asking twice.

Alan spent the next seven years with City, before moving on to take up coaching
posts with Blackpool, West Brom and Nottingham Forest. Last season, he returned to
his roots, taking on the chief scout's post at Rotherham.

Alan lives in the Midlands with wife Ann. They have a son (Alex) and a daughter
(Sally).

Alan heads for goal in a City game.

Alan Crawford today, with daughter Sally.

RICHARD DRYDEN

Most football fans have, at one time or another, picked their 'dream team' – a side made up of their footballing heroes. Former City man Richard Dryden could pick his own dream team, based on managers that he's played for. 'If you could put Glenn Hoddle, Joe Jordan, Terry Cooper, Bobby Gould, Gerry Francis, Graeme Souness, Peter Shilton and John McGovern in the same line-up, you'd be well on the way to having a good side,' he pointed out.

Spotted playing youth football by Bristol Rovers, Richard joined 'The Pirates' on a one-year training scheme. After making his debut as a 17-year-old, he went on to have two years as a full time pro with Rovers, making 13 league appearances. 'I moved on to Exeter City, managed by Terry Cooper. Apart from my parents, he was the single biggest influence on my career,' he said. Playing left back or left wing, Richard went on to make 92 appearances for the club. He also had a loan spell with Manchester City, but instead of joining them, he went to Notts County.

'County were a top-flight club at the time, having had two successive promotion seasons under Neil Warnock,' explained Richard. Now Neil probably wouldn't stake a claim to be in many people's dream team as a player, but, as Richard pointed out, as a manager, he was a great motivator.

Richard spent two years with County, during which time he went to Plymouth Argyle on loan to get match fit after injury. 'Shilton and McGovern were the management team there and you can only have respect for what they achieved as players.'

With County relegated from the old First Division, the chance to link up again with Cooper at Birmingham was too good to turn down. 'There were lots of good reasons to go to Birmingham, Terry [Cooper] not being the least of them.'

After half a hundred or so games for Brum, Richard moved back to Bristol, signing for City, managed at that time by Joe Jordan. 'It was great to be back in Bristol, but I have to say, it wasn't the best time of my career,' admitted Richard. 'I wasn't on top of my game and the fact that I'd played for Rovers didn't exactly make me a favourite with some fans.'

But, despite the negative attitude of a few and, by his own admission, some inconsistency in his game, Richard played around 40 games for The Robins between 1994 and '96. And when he did leave, it was to move back to the top flight with Southampton, although his time there was blighted by injury.

'I went out on loan to Stoke, Northampton and Swindon, but injuries had taken their toll and I'd lost some of my old pace,' he admitted. It was while he was at Stoke that he came on as a substitute in the Auto Windscreens Final at Wembley against City, to help Stoke win 2-1.

Next stop was Luton Town, but when they were relegated to the Third Division, Richard left for non-league Scarborough. He moved on to Worksop Town and had over two years as assistant to former team mate Mark Cooper, who was managing Tamworth.

These days, Richard, who lives in Nottingham with wife Lindsay and their young children Sam, Bethany and Charlie, is involved in the transport business.

Richard during his playing days.

Richard Dryden today, with two of his youngsters – Bethany and Sam.

JOHN EMMANUEL

'I was just a painter and decorator from 'The Valleys' who got the chance to become a footballer and took it.' So summed up John Emmanuel, who played 140 games for Bristol City, between 1971 and 1976, and was a member of the squad that kicked off their big promotion-winning season in '75/76.

Born in Treherbert, South Wales, John was playing in midfield for a local amateur side when he was spotted by a City scout. 'I was invited for a trial and arrived at Temple Meads with a bit of paper with the bus numbers to Ashton Gate written on it,' recalled John. 'It was all very different for me – back home one bus took you anywhere!'

Already a Welsh amateur international with four caps, John's trial period went well and, after appearing in a couple of reserve games, was selected to play against Rovers, in the annual end-of-season event between the two clubs, the Gloucester Cup Final.

'There was a very big crowd, but I did OK and I signed for City straight after, as I recall, in the toilets!'

The start of the 71/72 season saw John make his league debut for City in the opening fixture, a 3-3 draw with Millwall at Ashton Gate. He played in the next 18 consecutive games, scoring the first of his 10 goals for the club in his second match, a 5-1 win at Sheffield Wednesday. By the end of the season he had made 34 senior starts.

'I was twenty-three years old and had just got married, so to give up my job was quite a gamble, but, at the same time, the club had taken a gamble on signing me,' reasoned John, whose surname and background soon earnt him the nickname of 'Ivor' – after the Welsh singer of the same surname. 'I was very raw and had to learn quick – and I did.'

The following season John added another 38 senior appearances to his cv and picked up the prestigious Player of the Year award. In 73/74 and 74/75 another 30+ games each season, as well as two full caps for his country.

Although John played in three of the first four games of the 75/76 season, he found himself out of the side at the end of August. As the team began its ultimate push for promotion to the top level, manager Alan Dicks rarely changed his line-up. It was during that season that John had loan spells at Swindon and later Gillingham. He was to make his last City appearance in a 4-1 win over Oxford.

'Although I only played a handful of games in the big promotion season, I was very proud to have been part of City's success,' said John.

Having been released by City, John returned to Wales, enjoying two seasons with Fourth Division Newport County, before leaving league football.

'I'd had knee ligament problems towards the end of my career and was never quite the same player,' admitted John, who went on to play for Barry Town and Ton Pentre, where he was to spend many years as player/coach and later manager.

Off the soccer field, John worked as a clerical officer for the National Coal Board, before joining a kitchen manufacturing company.

Married to Jessica, the couple live in Mid Glamorgan and have two daughters.

'Thanks to Alan Dicks sticking his neck out in signing a raw lad from The Rhondda, I have a lot of great memories,' summed up John.

Bristol City's pre-season team photo, August 1975, with John, second from the right in the second row.

John today.

STEVE GALLIERS

Over the years, much has been said about the rise and fall of Wimbledon Foot-ball Club. Their meteoric climb from the Southern League into the Football League and then gaining First Division (now Premiership) status in less than 10 years, not to mention a certain FA Cup Final win, was nothing short of a fairy story. One man who was part of that adventure and rose with them up the Divisions, is former City captain Steve Galliers.

'I was playing non-league football for Chorley when Wimbledon came in for me,' recalled Steve. 'Wimbledon had just got into the Football League and their manager remembered me from when I had played against them.'

Once described as 'a pocket battleship', Steve was to prove a dominant force in 'The Dons' midfield, as he went on to notch up nearly 500 games for the club, as it astounded the football pundits by reaching the top flight in 1986. 'I also had a short spell with Crystal Palace in 1981, but was back at Wimbledon less than a year later,' he pointed out.

In February 1987, City moved to bring Steve to Bristol, initially on loan, and he soon made his presence felt in The Robins midfield, playing the last nine league games of the season and helping the club win their two-legged semi-final over Aldershot, to reach the final of the Freight Rover Trophy for a second successive year.

'Unfortunately, I got injured and missed the final,' said Steve, who underwent a cartilage operation and returned to Wimbledon. He wasn't away long though. One game into the start of the new season and he was heading back to Ashton, having done more than enough during his loan spell for the club to organise a permanent transfer.

'There were some very good people and some great players at City,' said Steve, who went on to complete 44 games for City in a season that saw them just miss out in the Play Offs, with Steve contributing five goals to the cause.

After their near-miss in the Play Offs the previous season, City started the new season (88/89) in optimistic mood. In the end, though, they had to settle for a disap-pointing eleventh position, although they did enjoy a healthy run in the Littlewoods Cup, bowing out in a tight two-legged semi final to Nottingham Forest. Steve made no fewer than 50 senior appearances that season, to take his City tally past the 100 mark, many of them as captain. Nevertheless, he was off at the start of the following season.

'I had the offer of a two-year contract with Maidstone United, who had just come up into the league from the Conference,' explained Steve. But what should have been the start of a new challenge turned sour for him. 'I had one injury after another and played just a handful of games,' he said. 'In fact, I spent the second year there as youth team coach.'

With injuries taking their toll – Steve went on to have both hips replaced in 2003 – Steve walked away from soccer. 'I've had a few jobs since then,' he said. 'I worked for a petrol company, was in telephone marketing, had a spell with The Office of Fair Trading and later became a postroom supervisor at Richmond-upon-Thames College.'

Appropriately enough, given his background, Steve lives just a few hundred yards from where the reborn Wimbledon – AFC Wimbledon – play their home games.

Steve during his time in City's midfield.

Steve Galliers today.

MARK GAVIN

He could send in centres with pin-point accuracy, just as regularly as he can pick a winner in the three-thirty, though without using a pin – that's former City winger Mark Gavin, who swapped the sport of soccer for the sport of kings. 'I'm what's called a professional gambler,' explained Mark.

Born in Lanarkshire, Mark began his footballing career with Leeds United, playing 30 first team games between 1982 and 1984. He also had a seven-game spell on loan at Hartlepool, before joining Carlisle United. Equally at home on either wing, Mark then had a couple of seasons with Bolton Wanderers, playing 49 games, including the match against City in the 1986 Freight Rover Final at Wembley.

'That was my first real encounter with Bristol City,' said Mark, who gave City full back Rob Newman an uncomfortable first half, before City ran out 3-nil winners.

After Bolton, Mark moved on to Rochdale – 23 games – before heading north of the border to Heart of Midlothian. His wing play had not gone unnoticed and, having caught the eye of City manager Joe Jordan, he came to Ashton Gate in 1988 for a fee of £35,000. 'I had no qualms about coming to Bristol,' said Mark, who made a dream start for The Robins by capping his first appearance in a City shirt with a goal less than two minutes into his debut. 'Jimmy Lumsden, who was Joe's number two, had been the assistant manager at Leeds during my time there, and that was a major factor. Also, I felt that the club was going places.'

Mark was to make over 40 appearances in his first season at Ashton Gate and the following year, City's promotion year, he passed the 50 mark, scoring five goals but, more importantly, laying on many of the 30+ goals netted that season by 'Super Bob' Taylor. 'That was a great season,' said Mark.

A dispute over new terms saw Mark leave Ashton Gate for Watford, City receiving £100,000 and Wayne Allison in exchange. But Mark was to play only 13 games for The Hornets. 'Looking back, going to Watford was a mistake, it was not a good move for me,' he admitted.

With Jimmy Lumsden now in the manager's chair, Mark returned to City at Christmas 1991, the club paying out £60,000 to bring the winger back to Bristol. He went on to make another 50 appearances, taking his City tally past the 150 mark, before departing for Terry Cooper's Exeter early in 1994.

'I think I played some of my best football at Exeter. Terry [Cooper] was brilliant, but the problem was that the club was potless,' said Mark. Around two seasons and 80 games on, Mark was on the move again, this time to Scunthorpe. 'If I'm honest, I was starting to wind down and had lost a bit of pace,' he admitted.

A short return to Hartlepool in the 1997/8 season marked the end of Mark's professional playing days, before he turned his back on goalposts and concentrating on winning posts.

Married to Joanne, the couple live in Hartlepool and have a son, Tom, and daughter Beth.

A look back shows that Mark played over 400 senior games for his respective clubs, netting 27 goals. But one thing is for certain. Winger Mark Gavin made countless goals for his team mates – and you can bet your mortgage on that.

Mark Gavin as a player for Bolton Wanderers.
(photo: *Bolton News*)

A more recent photo of Mark, with wife Joanne.

MIKE GIBSON

He may be a bit on the short side for a goalkeeper – five feet nine – but for many, Mike Gibson stands head and shoulders above the rest as the best goalie ever to don the keeper's jersey at Ashton Gate.

Mike was to play nearly 400 games for The Robins between 1963 and 1972 and was a vital member of the side that won promotion to the (old) Second Division in 1965. And yet, Mike was originally brought in as goalkeeping cover.

'I'd served an apprenticeship as an engineer with British Rail, and was playing part time when Shrewsbury spotted me,' said Mike. 'My first reaction was that if I could have a year or so doing something I really enjoyed, I should go for it.'

In his three seasons with 'The Shrews', Mike was to make over 100 senior appearances. It was towards the end of the 62/63 season that City manager Fred Ford went to watch 'Gibbo', as he sought to fill the void left by an injury to regular keeper Tony Cook. He saw enough to splash out £5,000 to sign Mike.

'Fred was a character and the most honest man I've ever met in the game, before or since,' said Mike. 'He could be quite fiery when the occasion demanded, but never held a grudge and was straight as a die.'

Mike made his debut in a home draw with Crystal Palace in May and by the following September had made the position his own. After finishing fifth that season, City stepped up a gear to win promotion the following year, with Mike an ever present. 'We went on a tremendous run that season,' recalled Mike. 'The crunch came when we faced my old team Shrewsbury in two matches in April.'

City showed their promotion credentials by hammering 'The Shrews' 5-1 away and then winning the home fixture 3-nil. 'My best mate at Shrewsbury was a guy called Peter Dolby,' went on Mike. 'He was marking 'Big John' [Atyeo] and John got four of the goals at their ground and another at Ashton Gate.'

Having enjoyed a fantastic run in to the end of the season, City needed to win their last home game, against Oldham, to go up. After a nervous start, City came through with a 2-nil win to spark scenes of jubilant celebrations amongst the 28,000 fans crammed into the ground. 'A wonderful memory,' said Mike.

And it was so nearly a second successive promotion year, when, despite playing against better opposition, the team just missed out on winning a place in the top flight.

After that first near-promotion miss City struggled and, in 1967, after another poor start, manager Ford was dismissed. 'The players were absolutely gutted when Fred was sacked,' said Mike.

Despite the change in management, with Alan Dicks' arrival, Mike was still virtually an ever present for the next three years, but, by February '72, emerging goalkeeper Ray Cashley had taken over the number one spot. '"Cash" had come in and done well,' said Mike philosophically. And, after leaving City in the summer of '72, Mike had his swan song by winning promotion with Gillingham.

After retiring at the end of the 73/74 season, Mike was, for many years, City's goalkeeping coach, ran a keep-fit programme, and travelled all over the country to assess City's opposition. All that and his 'day job' as a postie.

Married to Ann, the couple have two daughters and six grandchildren and live in the Uplands area of Bristol.

City keeper Mike Gibson.

Mike at home in Bristol.

SHAUN GOATER

Former City striker Shaun Goater is a man who started in very humble beginnings, went on to establish himself as a top striker and has since returned to his roots to give the youngsters back in Bermuda something to strive for.

It was nearly 20 years ago that Shaun was spotted playing for a Bermuda Select XI by Manchester United. A trial at Old Trafford followed, before Shaun was given a two-year contract and the chance to establish himself at one of Britain's biggest clubs. But it wasn't all plain sailing. Shaun had to combat homesickness, the English climate and missing his girlfriend (now his wife) Anita. There was also the small matter of the huge competition for places in Britain's leading side.

'There were so many established stars at United that I realised that if I was going to make it in England, I would have to move on. Not that that stopped me from learning from the great players and coaches at Old Trafford,' he pointed out. And so, in 1989, Shaun signed for Rotherham United.

Shaun was to score 86 goals in 262 appearances for 'The Millers', but, after seven years with the club, felt he needed a new challenge. That new challenge came in the form of Bristol City and after a fee of £175,000 had been agreed, Shaun signed on the dotted line. 'They were a good bunch of lads at Bristol and they made me feel at home straight away.'

Although Shaun's first game resulted in a 3-2 defeat, he marked his debut with a goal and the fans took to him very quickly, giving him the nickname 'Billy', as he continued to find the net on a regular basis. His first season at Ashton Gate saw the club make it to the Play Off semi-finals, before manager Joe Jordan departed, to be replaced by John Ward. 'John was one of the best managers I ever played under,' summed up Shaun.

Under Ward's guidance, the team was heading for automatic promotion. Shaun was scoring goals for fun – he had notched up 45 during his time at Ashton Gate – when Manchester City came in with a huge offer, just before the transfer deadline. 'Leaving Bristol was sad and I would have been happy to stay, had it not been for the chance of a move to a club like Manchester City.'

To go through Shaun's five seasons with Man City would take the best part of a book. His goal-scoring success at the club – 103 goals in 211 games – inspired the fans to come up with the chant 'Feed the Goat and he will Score.'

In 2003 Shaun was awarded the MBE for services to sport and young people in Bermuda, having organised soccer camps for the youngsters there since 1992. That same year he left Manchester for Reading, had 43 games for 'The Royals' and six on loan at Coventry, before ending his career at Southend United, helping the club to a second successive promotion. Ironically, his last game was against Bristol City, with both sets of fans applauding 'The Goat' along with over 100 Manchester City fans, who had made the trip to Roots Hall just to say 'cheerio' and 'thank you'.

'I do miss England, but I'm enjoying these new challenges,' summed up Shaun, now living in Bermuda with Anita and their two daughters.

An early City shot of Shaun.

Ready for a book signing session in Bristol.

47

GERRY GOW

'Football legends' – a phrase often over-used to describe soccer players. But Gerry Gow can rightly claim his place in the hall of fame at Ashton Gate. A tigerish midfield player, he made his Bristol City debut at 17, went on to skipper the side, helped the club win promotion to the top flight and became a firm favourite at City.

Glasgow-born Gerry made the long journey south with fellow young Scots Tom and Steve Ritchie. 'I'd always dreamed of being a professional footballer, so wasn't at all phased by going to Bristol,' said Gerry.

After making his debut in the final game of the 1969/70 season, Gerry became a regular in the side. 'There were some very good players at Ashton Gate when I arrived, including Bobby Kellard, a very similar player to myself.'

In fact, Gerry was to replace the experienced Kellard in City's side, as manager Alan Dicks set about building his team. 'Alan was a brilliant manager, who wanted his teams to play football and was very good for my career,' pointed out Gerry.

Between 1969 and 1980, Gerry was to experience plenty of highs, playing around 500 games for the club as they transformed from a team continually fighting relegation, to one that finally reached the top. 'Lots of great memories,' said Gerry. 'Obviously winning promotion, beating Arsenal away, knocking Leeds United out of the FA Cup on their own ground and, of course, that historic game at Coventry – a draw that ensured both clubs stayed up.'

But, at the end of the 79/80 season, the club lost their top-flight status. Struggling in the Second Division, Dicks lost his job and the writing was on the wall. 'The club was in trouble, on and off the field,' explained Gerry. 'Bob Houghton came in, but we didn't see eye to eye over tactics and that has to mean a parting of the ways.'

And so, just 13 games into the 80/81 season, Gerry headed back to the top division, City having accepted much needed funds in the form of a large transfer fee from Manchester City. Gerry was to play around 30 games for the Maine Road side, including the FA Cup Final marathon with Spurs. 'It's every footballer's dream to play in the FA Cup Final at Wembley and, even though we lost [after a replay] it was a great experience.'

After Man City, Gerry moved to Rotherham, managed by the late Emlyn Hughes. 'Emlyn was a brilliant bloke. I couldn't believe it when he died,' said Gerry.

After 58 games for Rotherham, Gerry moved on to play nine times for Burnley, but he knew he was nearing the end of his playing days. 'To be honest, the knees had started to go,' he admitted.

The chance to move back south and become player manager at Yeovil Town was too good to resist for the Scot. 'It was quite a challenge,' admitted Gerry. 'The club were bottom of the Conference and skint. I managed to steady the ship and turn things around.'

After Yeovil, Gerry quit soccer to run a pub, just up the road from the City ground, but returned to the game to take over the hot seat at Weymouth. 'That was how I came to settle in Dorset,' explained Gerry, who has three children and seven grandchildren.

After a year managing Weymouth, Gerry tried a variety of jobs, before joining an engineering firm two or three years ago.

A young Gerry Gow in his City days.

A more recent picture of Gerry.

MICK HARFORD

As a centre forward never afraid to go in where it hurts, Mick Harford has never shirked a challenge in his life. In a playing career spanning more than 20 years, he has played against some of the toughest defenders in all four divisions, notching up over 700 games, scoring 233 goals and picking up two England caps along the way. But the striker, who had seven months at Bristol City during his travels, had a challenge and a half on his hands, managing a Luton Town side that started the 2008/9 season on minus 30 points.

'Obviously it was a very tough situation,' admitted Mick. 'The club had gone into administration because of the mismanagement of people who've since left and it was everyone left at the club after their departure who suffered.'

Long before he accepted what many would call 'mission impossible,' Mick started off in professional football with Third Division Lincoln City. 'I was a plumber playing for Lambton Boys Club when Lincoln's then manager, Graham Taylor, signed me.'

Mick spent three years with 'The Imps,' but his knack of finding the back of the net – he scored 41 league goals in the old Third and Fourth divisions – meant that he was destined for one of the big clubs. Newcastle United duly obliged, paying out £180,000 for his services in December 1980.

'Although born in Sunderland and a 'Black Cats' supporter as a kid, I was delighted to be going to such a big club, although the move probably came a little too soon for me, but I learnt a lot during my time there,' said Mick.

In the summer of 1981, unaware of the financial time bomb ticking away at Bristol City, Mick agreed a move to come to Ashton Gate, where the team's tumble down the divisions was to prove the least of their worries. Even his £160,000 transfer fee was being paid on the 'never never'.

'Although City had suffered two relegations, they were – still are – a big club and it seemed a good opportunity for me,' he said. Mick made the perfect start to his time with The Robins, winning instant favour with a goal in each of his first two games. 'I was living in Clifton with Gary Mabbutt in the flat above and we became good friends,' recalled Mick.

Despite Mick's performances on the field, the team continued to slide down the table. Worse still, they had gone into financial meltdown, culminating in the departure of the Ashton Gate Eight. 'What those lads did to ensure City's survival was tremendous and I have the utmost respect for them,' he pointed out.

Mick was a member of what could have been the club's last-ever league game that dark day in January '82, scoring their goal in a one-all draw at Newport. Two months later, after 40 games and 14 goals for The Robins, he was sold to Birmingham City.

Over the next 14 years, Mick would go on to make his mark at Luton Town (twice), Derby County, Chelsea (he scored their first ever Premiership goal), his home town club (Sunderland) and Coventry City, before winding up his playing days with Wimbledon.

After calling it a day on playing, Mick had spells on the staff at Wimbledon, Luton, Nottingham Forest, Swindon, Rotherham and QPR, in either coaching or management, before returning once again to Luton, with the impossible task of trying to preserve The Hatters' league status.

Mick in playing days action.

A life of challenges for Mick Harford.

NIGEL HAWKINS

If you're looking for a 'good runner' then former Bristol City striker Nigel Hawkins is your man. Not only does he enjoy taking part in marathons, but he is also a company director at a large motor company in Thornbury.

'It's a family concern and I've been involved since about 1994,' said Nigel, adding that his grandfather founded the business way back in 1927.

Prior to his move into the car business, Nigel had set out to pursue a career as a professional footballer. Born in Bristol, he joined City as an apprentice in 1986. 'Terry Cooper was manager at the time, although it was Joe Jordan who gave me my first-team debut, early in the 1988/89 season,' recalled Nigel.

By the end of that season Nigel had featured in 23 senior games, either starting or as a playing substitute and had netted three goals. 'My first was a header against Oxford in the Littlewoods Cup, the second, another header, was the winner against Reading and my last goal for City came against Cardiff in the league,' said Nigel.

But, with competition fierce for places in City's attack, Nigel decided to move on in order to get regular first-team football. 'Bob Taylor and Robbie Turner were leading the line and my chances appeared limited,' he explained. A fee of around £18,000 saw him depart for Blackpool. But the move was not the success he was hoping for, as injuries and a change of managers saw him restricted to around 20 games in his three years at the Bloomfield Road club.

'After City, Blackpool was a real culture shock,' he admitted. 'With hindsight, I should have stuck it out a bit longer at Ashton Gate.'

An operation for cruciate knee ligament damage meant 18 months on the sidelines and, in a bid to get fit, he went to Bath City on loan. 'That was a disaster, as I lasted just twenty minutes and got knocked out,' he said. 'It was only thanks to the prompt action of the Bath physio, who realised that I'd swallowed my tongue, that I'm here today.'

Out of contract at Blackpool, Nigel returned home and played Southern League football for Weston-super-Mare. 'I managed about a season and a half for them, but even at that level, my leg wouldn't stand up to the rigours of competitive matches,' he pointed out.

But, with sport very much in his blood stream, Nigel took up marathon running and Tai Kwando. 'I completed the Kilimanjaro Marathon in 2006,' he said proudly. 'I'm OK with sports that don't involve any sudden twisting or turning and I often take part in local marathons with my girlfriend Diana,' he added.

But running was put on hold early in 2008, as Nigel went into hospital for an exploratory operation on his knee – a legacy of being a professional footballer.

'A footballer's life is all about "what ifs" and "if onlys" and things like injuries you have no real control of, they're part and parcel of most players' lives,' he summed up.

Nigel in action for Bristol City.

In the driving seat as a director at Berkeley Vale Motors.

MATT HEWLETT

W hen you set off on a career as a professional footballer, the one thing you can't really cater for is a career-threatening injury. Sadly, former City midfield star Matt Hewlett has had to wrap up his soccer career for that very reason. And, instead of delivering defence splitting passes, he's now delivering a wide range of snacks and foodstuffs, as he embarks on a new career in catering.

'As a player, I was always ambitious to succeed and, although I'm very disappointed at having to quit, I'm grateful that I managed to play the number of games that I did,' said Matt, who can nowadays be found at Scoffers, the family catering business in Pucklechurch.

Born in the St George area of Bristol, Matt came up from the junior ranks with City, alongside the likes of Tommy Doherty and Louis Carey. He went on to make his debut at Wolves in 1993, aged 17. 'Russell Osman gave me my big chance and, although we lost, I really enjoyed the moment – you never forget your first senior game,' he pointed out. He also went on to represent England Under-18s and was later on stand by for the national Under-21s side.

At the end of that first season Matt had made 14 senior appearances. Over the next eight years he played under a further four managers, appearing in a total of 154 senior games and scoring 12 times. Sandwiched in between, he also had short loan spells with Bath City and Burnley.

In 1996, Matt experienced the disappointment of losing out in the Play Offs, having been practically an ever present in the side. But that was forgotten when, under John Ward, the club won promotion to the First Division (now the Championship) the following year, with Matt's name one of the first on the team sheet each week.

The new season saw City desperately trying to stave off relegation, but to no avail and City went back to the division they'd come up from the year before. Bad form by the team as a whole, a change of management and tactical changes that never really worked, did nothing to help Matt's confidence and a change of clubs seemed to be the best solution.

In July 2000 Swindon Town came in for Matt. 'It was a good move for me as I had a better chance of regular first-team football and, because it was Swindon, I didn't have to move,' he said. Colin Todd and Andy King were the management team at Town and over the next five years, Matt enjoyed around 200 appearances in Swindon's colours.

In the summer of 2005, Matt signed for Torquay United and moved down to Devon. He went on to make a couple of dozen appearances for them, but his career with 'The Gulls' was cruelly cut short by injury.

'I had a prolapsed disc and, despite surgery, I was told that I'd have to quit professional football,' said Matt. 'I was really gutted, because it meant the end of a football career and the fans at Torquay hadn't really had the chance to see the best of me.'

And so, just a few games short of the 400 mark, Matt made a complete switch from soccer, teaming up with brother James in the family catering business.

Married to Rachel, the couple live in Downend and have a young son, Calum.

Matt in action for City.

Matt loads up the van ready for
the sandwich run, with brother
James in the front.

CHRIS HONOR

Like it or hate it, the Bosman Ruling completely changed the way clubs bought and sold players. But for former City player Chris Honor, the ruling arrived too late to save a soccer career that was bogged down in legal wrangling, after his club refused to release him.

'I'd left City to play for Airdrieonians in 1991,' explained Chris. 'I was virtually an ever present for over three years, playing for them in the Scottish Cup Final, but wanted to move back into the English League.'

Chris's desire to return south was understandable. He had moved back to Bristol after living in Scotland for three years, was training at Ashton Gate during the week and flying up to Scotland on match days. 'It sounds crazy now, given the changes that Bosman brought about, but the club simply refused to let me go, even though I was out of contract.'

It had all started so differently for Chris, when he joined City as an apprentice in 1986. Equally at home in midfield or defence, he made his first team debut at 17. 'Terry Cooper was the manager and he was a fantastic guy to play for,' said Chris.

A broken leg temporarily put a halt to Chris' progress but, by the end of the 1989/90 season, he had notched up over 70 appearances for the team. 'We won promotion and had a good run in the Littlewoods Cup, but by that time Joe Jordan had taken over and I didn't agree with a lot of his management style,' said Chris.

Needing a change, Chris was offered a contract with Airdrieonians. 'I kept putting them off as I knew Terry [Cooper] was probably going to be Birmingham's new boss and that he might want to sign me. I held out as long as I could, but in the end signed for Airdrie. It was a body blow when, the day after I'd signed, Terry was announced as Birmingham's new manager.'

At the start everything went well for Chris in Scotland. 'We moved up and I loved it there. It was a great experience, especially playing in front of crowds of 60,000 at Hampden and Ibrox,' recalled Chris.

But, after three years, Chris wanted to move back south. 'The club had been relegated, my wife was homesick and I knew it was time to leave,' he said. Airdrie didn't agree. 'I signed monthly contracts and moved back to Bristol. Russell Osman was very good, letting me train at City. It got to the ridiculous stage that Airdrie stopped paying me, but wouldn't release me.'

Supported by the PFA, Chris had the same solicitor who went on to represent Jean-Marc Bosman, but the situation dragged on. Eventually Chris got his freedom, but the two-and-a-half years he'd spent out of the game put paid to any hope of resurrecting a League career. And to add insult to injury, even though he won his case, Airdrie went bankrupt and Chris didn't receive a penny.

'When I did get my release, I had two spells with Bath City, plus four years with Forest Green Rovers, skippering them at Wembley in the final of the FA Trophy,' said Chris.

Away from football, Chris has run a petrol station and has also been involved in the property market. He lives in Redland with his wife Kirsty and the couple have two young daughters, Ita and Amelia.

Chris (back row, second from the right) in the City line up.

Chris today, working on one of his properties.

GLENN HUMPHRIES

Love or hate the once mighty Leeds United side that Don Revie moulded, many of the players from that team went on to make their mark in management. Former City centre half Glenn Humphries considers himself fortunate to have played for three of them.

'I'd been spotted playing in the Northern Premier League by Billy Bremner, who, at that time, was manager of Doncaster Rovers,' said Glenn. 'He signed me on and gave me my debut at sixteen. The club didn't have much money, but he did a marvelous job there.'

Glenn was to spend five years at Doncaster, playing over 200 senior games. 'When Billy left the side broke up, so when City manager Terry Cooper came in for me I jumped at the chance. I'd played alongside him at 'Donny' and knew he was a sound bloke. I'd also played at Ashton Gate a few times, so I knew it was a great ground with fantastic support.'

Looking back, Glenn vividly recalls the Play Off marathon with Walsall, when the club just missed out on promotion. 'We'd lost the first leg three-one at home and everyone had written us off. But we went to their place and got a two-nil win to level the aggregate. In fact, Carl [Shutt] missed a sitter right at the end that would have won it for us.'

The record books show that City finally lost the third deciding tie, but two years later, under the management of another former Leeds legend, Joe Jordan, they achieved their goal, finishing runners up to gain promotion.

'There were some good players at Ashton Gate,' said Glenn. 'Rob Newman, who could play anywhere; Alan Walsh, who had one hell of a shot; 'Louie' [Andy Llewellyn] who never shirked a tackle; 'Gav' [Mark Gavin] who supplied inch-perfect centres and Bob Taylor – what a striker!'

But, although the club had won promotion and everything was looking good, Glenn, who had played over 100 games for The Robins, was to move on. 'I was pretty much settled in Bristol, but my wife Joanne was homesick. I didn't really want to leave, but family must come first,' he explained. 'The club was very good about it and helped me get a move back up north to Scunthorpe.'

With Glenn in the heart of the defence, Scunthorpe made the Play Offs two years running, without success. 'The manager, Bill Green, wasn't given the funds to make it work and when he got the sack, I decided it was time to go as well.'

Glenn was to spend four months with non-league Frickley, before flying off to Hong Kong to play for Golden Valley. 'I was out there nearly three years. There were a lot of ex-pats playing there and it was a fantastic experience.'

On his return to England Glenn was considering an offer to play in Australia, when Hull City offered him a contract. 'It was my home town and I'd been training with them. I knew my playing days were nearly over, so it seemed appropriate to finish my career there.'

And so, a league career of nearly 400 games wound down at Hull, with Glenn having a season in non-league football, before a broken bone in his foot meant hanging up the boots. Employed by a mobile homes manufacturer, Glenn lives in Hull with his wife. They have twin sons Glenn (junior) and Lee.

Glenn in his City days with sons Glenn (junior) and Lee as match day mascots.

A recent picture of Glenn and his family.

STEVE JOHNSON

'It's probably just one of life's little ironies, but I always played better against City, than I did playing for them.' That was how former Robins striker Steve Johnson initially summed up his time at Bristol City.

Born in Liverpool, Steve had worked as a French polisher, before making the grade as a footballer. It was while he was playing in a trial match for Altrincham that he got his big break. 'We were playing a pre-season friendly against Bury, who were in the old Third Division. I recall having a good game that day and the Bury manager must have thought so as well, because he offered me a contract.'

Over the next six years, Steve was to make nearly 200 appearances for 'The Shakers', scoring 52 league goals. 'I enjoyed my time at Gigg Lane, but had a falling out with my last manager there and decided to move on.'

Steve got a transfer to Rochdale, but the team struggled and after around 20 games he left to join the league new boys, Wigan Athletic. Over one-and-a-half seasons, Steve played some 60 games for the side.

Traditionally a club which, in those days, needed to cash in on their better players, Wigan found a £40,000 Bristol City bid for Steve's services too good to refuse. And so, in March 1985, Steve made the move to join Terry Cooper's City side. 'City was – still is – a big club and when I joined them they had some class players, like Keith Curle. Also, there was Alan Walsh – what a shot he had! We used to fight over trying to take the free kicks.'

Steve's City career started well, as he scored on his full debut in a 2-nil win over Hull City at Ashton Gate and found the net again two weeks later in a 2-2 draw with his old team Wigan. But, after so long in the north, it was always going to be a struggle for Steve to adjust. 'It was so frustrating,' he admitted. 'City were the biggest club I'd played for, but I just couldn't settle. My wife Angela was pregnant at the time and didn't really want to move to Bristol and in the end I was commuting up and down from Bury, which is not ideal.'

One of the best in man-management, Terry Cooper sympathised with Steve's problem. 'Terry was great,' said Steve. 'He arranged for me to go on loan back to Rochdale and also to Chester City, before I got a permanent transfer to Scunthorpe.'

And so, after a return of five goals from 23 games, Steve left City. 'As soon as I was back up north with my family I started to enjoy my football again,' pointed out Steve, who went on to play around 80 games, scoring 20 league goals.

In the summer of '88 Steve had a season back at Chester City, before plying his trade overseas with Swedish club Huskvana, followed by a third and final spell with Rochdale.

After Rochdale, Steve played for Cork City in Ireland, before returning to Lancashire to finish his playing days in non-league football. Off the pitch he has worked in insurance and for the past 13 years has been with an industrial belt manufacturer in Bury.

Married to Angela, the couple live in Bury and have a daughter – Jamie Lee.

Steve in his City days.

Steve today with wife Angela and daughter Jamie Lee.

JOE JORDAN

Where do you start with Joe Jordan? Here is a man who has played football at the highest level, both in this country and overseas. Someone who has commanded record transfer fees, played over half a century of games for his country, been inducted into Scottish football's Hall of Fame and finished his playing days in City's red and white, not to mention twice managing the club.

Born in Lanarkshire, he played in the Scottish League for Greenock Morton, moving to Leeds United in 1971. After over 200 appearances, he signed for Manchester United for a record transfer fee of £350,000. In 1981 he headed to Italy, enjoying successful spells at AC Milan and Verona, before returning home to join Southampton. Along the way, he won 52 caps for Scotland, becoming the first Scottish player to score in three World Cup tournaments.

In 1987, former Leeds team mate Terry Cooper, then managing Bristol City, got in touch, with a view to Joe joining him. 'I didn't jump at the offer, but Terry was a good salesman and I agreed to come on loan,' said Joe.

After his initial loan period he was offered a permanent contract and later stepped up to become player/coach/assistant manager. And, when Cooper departed, the Board turned to Joe. 'I was offered the job on a caretaker basis and got the team to the Play Off finals,' recalled Joe.

Although City lost in the Play Offs, Joe had done enough to earn a two-year contract. In his first full season as manager, City finished eleventh in the (old) Third Division, but the following year Joe achieved his goal – promotion.

Early in the 90/91 season Scottish club Hearts asked Joe to be their manager. Despite an excellent record with them, the chairman decided to dispense with Joe's services, shortly before the end of his third season. 'Looking back I still feel a little bitter about that,' said Joe. 'Bearing in mind the Celtic and Rangers dominance, we had led the Scottish league for a while, qualified for Europe, our youth team had won the Scottish Youth Cup and our reserves had won their league.'

After Hearts, Joe became Liam Brady's number two at Celtic. But, with Celtic playing catch-up with leaders and great rivals Rangers, Liam resigned. 'I didn't think it was right to take over from him, so I left as well,' said Joe.

Joe was soon back in management, taking over at Stoke City, but when Lou Macari was ousted from Celtic, Stoke sacrificed Joe to give Lou his old job back.

In a strange twist of fate, Joe found himself back at Bristol City. 'I returned in the November,' said Joe. 'The team was bottom of the (old) Second Division and although they battled well, we went down.'

Joe's second spell at Ashton Gate – three years – didn't bring the success he'd achieved the first time round and ended in him leaving again. After City, Joe covered Italian soccer for television, was coach for the Northern Ireland team and then assistant manager at Huddersfield Town. In more recent years he was part of the Portsmouth coaching staff under Harry Redknapp. The pair worked well together, bringing success to the South Coast club, before they left to continue their partnership with Spurs.

Married to Judith, the couple have two daughters, Lucy and Caroline, and two sons (and former professional footballers) Andrew and Tom.

Joe Jordan in action.

Coach Joe Jordan.
(photo: *The News*, Portsmouth)

MARTIN KUHL

If it hadn't have been for a two-year spell playing in Hong Kong, former City midfield star Martin Kuhl may never have gone into coaching. 'We had a Brazilian trainer who really opened my eyes to so many different aspects of football coaching, that I realised this was the way I wanted to go with my career,' he said.

Martin had arrived at Bristol City in December 1994, having spent the previous 12 years in the old First and Second divisions, with half a dozen clubs.

It was while he was with his first club, Birmingham City, that Martin met someone who could certainly put punch in any strike force – legendary boxer Muhammad Ali. 'He was visiting the area to promote the Muhammad Ali Centres and he came into our dressing room before a match,' explained Martin. 'No outsiders were ever allowed in the home dressing room before a game – but this was Muhammad Ali. I shook his hand and got an autograph.'

After 132 appearances for The Blues, Martin moved to Sheffield United in an exchange deal involving winger Steve Wigley. 'I had a year at Sheffield, then a short spell with Watford, before going on to spend five years with Portsmouth,' he said.

In 1992 Martin moved on to Derby County before, after a short loan spell with Notts County, he moved to Bristol.

'Joe Jordan signed me to help in the fight against relegation from what is now the Championship. I had a lot of admiration and respect for Joe and decided to sign for City.'

But, despite Martin arriving to reinforce the side, the team failed to avoid the drop. 'There were some very good players at the club, such as Junior Bent, Gary Owers and Mark Shail, but despite that, we went down,' he recalled. 'It didn't seem to matter how well we played, we couldn't get out of trouble and once you're on a losing streak like that, it becomes psychological and almost impossible to get out of.'

After relegation and Joe's subsequent departure, John Ward came in, guiding the team to the Play Offs. 'We were up against Brentford over two legs and simply didn't perform,' admitted Martin. 'It was tough losing out and to make matters worse, it was televised.' An ever present, Martin's skills and commitment earned him the respect of the fans and the coveted Player of the Year award.

Two years after joining City, Martin took up a new challenge, flying out to play in Hong Kong. 'That was a fantastic experience and I loved it there. We won the league, which was very nice, but it was the skills and methods of our Brazilian coach that got me thinking that perhaps that was where my future would be.'

Returning home, Martin had the chance of playing in The States. 'It was a very good offer, but I decided it was time to put my family first,' said Martin. 'My daughter had been to nine different schools in as many years and it was time for some stability.'

After spells with non-league Farnborough Town and Carshalton Athletic, Martin signed for Aldershot Town. As assistant manager, he helped guide the club back into the Football League

A fully qualified coach, Martin lives in Sandhurst with wife Sharon, teenage daughters Emily and Georgia and teenage son Aaron.

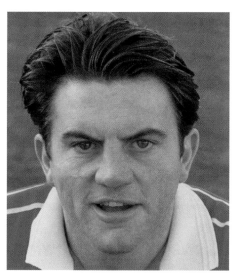

Martin in his playing days at City.

Martin Kuhl today.

JOHN KURILA

There are some players that stand out in a team. They have that certain something and even if they only play a handful of games for your side, they leave an impression. One such player was John Kurila, a wing half who came to City from Northampton Town, via Hamilton Steelers of Canada.

'I had an arrangement that I could go to Canada to play for Steelers in the summer,' said John. 'There was some mix up over my registration when I got back and I ended up signing for Bristol City.'

Born in Glasgow, John started off as a pro with the mighty Celtic. 'I played about half a dozen senior games for Celtic, including one of the derby matches against Rangers,' he recalled.

John had his first spell in Canada, before signing for Northampton Town in 1962. Practically an ever present in his first season with 'The Cobblers', he returned to Canada for summer soccer with The Steelers. On returning, though, he found that he could only go back to Northampton if they paid the Canadian side a fee – or he could talk to other clubs. 'Northampton weren't too happy about that and, at one time, I was on the verge of signing for Watford, but the deal fell through.'

And so John came to Ashton Gate. 'Fred Ford signed me for City – an excellent manager and a very nice man. I knew they had some very good players, like 'Shadow' Williams and Jantzen Derrick. And of course, there was the legend that was John Atyeo, who could do anything with a ball, despite the great big boots he used to wear.'

During his time with City, John became good friends with fellow Scotsman Gordon Low. 'When I came down I stayed with Gordon and we got on really well. A smashing bloke.'

One of the things that stood out, watching John play, was his reaction if he got fouled. None of this handbags at five paces stuff. He'd pick himself up, dust himself off, register who the culprit had been and bide his time. You knew that later on he'd even up the scores. Nothing malicious, just a 'that's the one I owe you for earlier' type of retribution.

Sadly for many City fans, John's stay with City was a short one. Just four months after joining The Robins, Northampton realised how much they missed him and promptly got their cheque book out to get him back.

John was to enjoy five seasons back with Northampton. 'I went up to the old First Division with them – the one and only time the club reached the top flight. A fantastic experience, though we ended up dropping back down again.'

A couple of seasons at Southend United followed and then, another 'high' for John, as his next club, Colchester United, made the headlines, by knocking the mighty Leeds United out of the FA Cup. 'I was driving to the game with team mate Ray Crawford, who was in the twilight of his career,' recalled John. 'Ray turned to me and said, "we'll be alright, I always play well against Jack Charlton." He went on to score twice in our three-two win.'

After Colchester, John had a season with Lincoln City, before dropping into non-league soccer. A self employed carpenter until his retirement, John lives in Northampton with his wife Nan. They have two sons, who both played professional football, a daughter, five grandchildren and a great grandson.

A youthful John Kurila in his early playing days.

A more recent picture of John (left), taken at a Northampton Old Boys reunion. (photos: Peter Norton Photography of Northampton)

ANDY LEANING

One easy way for a goalkeeper to become a hero with the fans at Bristol City is to save a penalty. And make that in a game against arch-rivals Rovers and you're guaranteed to be a hero for life, as former City keeper Andy Leaning discovered.

'It was nil-nil, with about five or six minutes to go, when Devon White was brought down,' recalled Andy. 'Ollie (Ian Holloway) took the penalty, but I managed to keep it out. Then we broke away and Louie Donowa scored the winner.

'We had a fantastic evening afterwards and I don't think I bought a drink all night!'

Born in Yorkshire, Andy didn't sign as a full-time pro until he was 22. 'I was determined to get a trade under my belt and served a joinery apprenticeship before I committed myself to soccer.'

Having served his apprenticeship, Andy signed with York City, where he was to spend two years and make around 70 appearances, before being transferred to Sheffield United. Unfortunately, his first season there saw United relegated to the (old) Third Division and his appearances restricted through injury.

It was while he was on the road to recovery that he got the call to join City. 'United's manager Dave Bassett told me City were interested in taking me on loan,' said Andy. 'It meant getting my match fitness back and first team action, so I went.'

With little chance to get to know his new team mates, Andy went straight into the side, less than 24 hours after signing. 'It was a cup game at Oxford. Joe [Jordan] said just go out and enjoy it. I did. We won and it felt good to be back.'

Andy's move to The Robins was made permanent and over the course of the next four years, he played in 80 senior games. 'I was originally brought in to cover for Keith Waugh, but after seven games I got injured,' he recalled.

Ironically, Andy suffered his injury saving a shot in training. 'I had some discomfort in my fingers, but got through the next couple of games with the help of pain killing injections,' said Andy. X-rays revealed he had been playing with a fractured finger. 'I went on the injured list just as Keith [Waugh] had recovered from his injury and he regained his place in the team.'

Waugh's departure for Coventry at the start of the 89/90 season gave Andy the chance to re-establish himself as the club's regular goalkeeper and he had a run of 22 games, before a ruptured thigh muscle meant another long lay off. Ronnie Sinclair stepped up to take over and Andy could only look on as City won promotion from the Third Division.

The beginning of the following season saw Andy and Ronnie competing for first-team selection, with Andy making 31 appearances. The arrival of Keith Welch from Rochdale in the summer of '91 saw Andy back on the sidelines, but he reclaimed his place in October and stayed in the side for the next 24 consecutive matches.

It was in March '94 that Andy left Ashton Gate for Lincoln, enjoying around 50 games for 'The Imps'. A move to Chesterfield followed two years later and he finished his playing days after four seasons there.

In 2003 Andy became Sheffield United's full-time goalkeeping coach. Married to Karen, the couple have a teenage son (Jack) and live in York.

Andy during his Bristol City days.

Words of wisdom from Andy
during a coaching session.

GORDON LOW

Bill Shankly gave him his league debut, he's good friends with the legendary Denis Law and he succeeded John Atyeo as captain of Bristol City, making over 200 appearances for the club. The person in question is Aberdeen-born Gordon Low.

Gordon moved to City from his first club, Huddersfield Town, in 1961. 'It was during Bill Shankly's time at Huddersfield that I made my debut,' said Gordon. 'The side had lost 7-6 the week before, so I guess he thought the defence needed tightening!' Gordon got off to a good start, and the defence certainly tightened up, winning one-nil against Middlesbrough.

But after nearly four years at Huddersfield and 67 senior appearances, Gordon needed a new challenge. 'I didn't really get on with the manager at the time, and took the chance to follow my old team mate and friend Jack Connor to Bristol.'

And so, in March 1961, Gordon was reunited with Jack, making his debut in a home win over Watford. Initially vying with Jack for the number five shirt, Gordon made seven appearances in the run in to that season, 29 appearances over the following two seasons, before establishing himself in the number six shirt.

At the end of the 1963/64 season Gordon made 38 appearances and the following season, the year of promotion from the (old) Third Division, he was an ever present. 'We had a really good side,' recalled Gordon. 'Mike Gibson in goal, Jack [Connor], Jantzen Derrick, who should have gone on to a big club, Gerry Sharpe and, of course John [Atyeo].'

And the club so nearly went straight up to the top flight. 'We had two crucial games against Southampton,' said Gordon. 'They beat us one-nil at Ashton in a game we could and should have won and then we were leading two-one at The Dell when they equalised deep into injury time. If we had won those two matches it would have been us instead of them going up. It was so disappointing,' he admitted.

The following season, with 'Big John' Atyeo having hung up his boots, Gordon took over the captaincy, missing just one game during the campaign. But the side struggled, finishing in fifteenth position and early the following season, with the team losing four games on the trot, manager Fred Ford was relieved of his post, to be succeeded by Alan Dicks.

'I loved it at Bristol, but when Fred went I knew it was time to move on,' said Gordon, sadly. And so he left Ashton Gate and moved on to Stockport County. 'My first season there we were doing well, but then the chairman decided to sell our two best strikers and it all went downhill,' he said.

After two seasons and 64 games for Stockport, Gordon had a brief spell with Crewe Alexandra, before leaving the professional soccer scene.

'After soccer I was a rep for a central-heating firm and then went on to work for a large toy manufacturers, covering the North of England,' said Gordon. 'I also spent fourteen years coaching youngsters, part-time, at Huddersfield,' he added.

Married to Brenda, the couple have four children (three boys and a girl) and live in Linthwaite in Huddersfield.

Gordon (second from the right) looks on anxiously as a City team mate clears.

Gordon Low (third from the left) at a Huddersfield Town Old Boys reunion, with Ray Wilson (left), Denis Law and Jack Connor.

JOHN MacPHAIL

When John MacPhail went to Sheffield United on a month's loan, he didn't really make much of an impression. In fairness, he didn't have much of a chance to. 'It was the time of the big freeze,' explained John, who would later feature for City. 'In the end, I spent three months there on loan before they could see enough of me to sign me on.'

Born in Dundee, John started off as an apprentice with his local club, where he spent five years, before moving south for his weather-enforced extended loan with Sheffield United in 1978. After signing permanently, he was to experience two relegations and a promotion there.

'I played over a hundred and fifty games for them and really enjoyed my time there,' said John. In February '83, John moved on to York City, managed by Denis Smith (later to manage City). He would later renew his working relationship with Denis, although that had looked impossible when the two fell out over his move to Bristol.

'I was virtually an ever present for York for three years and was looking for an improved contract,' explained John. 'The club wouldn't budge on their offer, so when I asked to transfer, the club valued me at £60,000. The case went to tribunal, City got me for £13,500 and Denis didn't speak to me for a year!'

Manager Terry Cooper snapped up the Scotsman for the reduced fee and John went on to establish himself in the heart of City's defence. Although they missed promotion that season, it was the experience of a trip to Wembley (Freight Rover Trophy Final) that gave John one of his best City memories. 'Some of the side were there the previous year when they beat Bolton, but I'd never been there before, not even as a spectator.'

City were to lose the match against Mansfield in the deciding penalty shoot out, although John, something of a penalty specialist during his career, confidently netted his spot kick.

In the summer of 1987, almost a year to the day that he'd signed for City, John was told that the club had received an offer for him. 'When they said it was from Denis Smith, who had moved on to Sunderland, I thought it was a joke,' laughed John. 'Given the fact that we'd fallen out over my move from York, I was very surprised.'

But the chance to join such a big club was too good to resist and John was to enjoy two promotions, from the Third to the First, during his time at Roker Park. He went on to play 153 games for the side, scoring 22 goals – many of them penalties.

In 1990, John moved to Fourth Division Hartlepool, where he spent five seasons, going on to become player-manager in November '93. 'Now that was an education,' said John. 'The club had no money and it was a thankless task.'

After ten months, John was relieved of his duties as manager, but the club retained his registration as a player. 'That was an impossible situation and I had to take legal advice to resolve it.'

John lives in the Stockton area and is married to Diane. They have two daughters, Charlotte and Kelly, and John has another daughter, Rebecca, from his first marriage. After soccer, John ran his own business installing kitchens, before going to work as a salesman for one of the area's major car retailers.

John in his City days.

A more recent photograph of John.

JIMMY MANN

It seems incredible that it is close on 30 years since the 'Ashton Gate Eight' walked away from the club to ensure that Bristol City lived on. One of the eight was Yorkshire-born Jimmy Mann.

Jimmy began his footballing career at Leeds United – probably the best club in the country at that time. 'They were an exceptional team, with exceptional players and a manager [Don Revie] second to none,' pointed out Jimmy, who lives in his birthplace in Goole.

The only trouble with being with such a good team is, of course, trying to break into the senior side. And with first-team chances few and far between – Jimmy made just two senior starts – he accepted the chance of joining Bristol City. 'There were one or two other clubs after me at the time, but I signed for City and my team mate John Shaw followed me down shortly after,' he said. 'The first problem I had when I arrived was learning the language!' he said with a laugh. 'No one could understand my Yorkshire accent and Bristolian was just as alien to me.'

Jimmy made his City debut at the start of the 74/75 season, away to Nottingham Forest and went on to make 32 appearances in his first season at the club. And it was against Forest a few years later that Jimmy entered City folklore with a 40-yard screamer past their England goalkeeper Peter Shilton. 'Fans often ask me about that one. Looking back, it was probably my best ever goal,' confessed Jimmy. 'I just caught it spot on and let fly and it beat Shilton all ends up and flew into the top corner of the net.'

Another highlight, of course, was the club gaining promotion to the top flight in 1976, with Jimmy virtually an ever present. 'Now that was a very special occasion,' he said.

Altogether Jimmy played nearly 300 senior games for The Robins, but then came the crash – with Jimmy entering the record books as one of the 'Ashton Gate Eight'. 'It was a disaster,' he confessed. 'The club was plummeting down the leagues and on the verge of bankruptcy. They very nearly went under.'

But the sacrifice that Jimmy and his seven colleagues made meant the club survived. Jimmy moved back to Yorkshire, signing for Norman Hunter's Barnsley. 'I didn't really enjoy it there, but you just have to get on with it, just like most other jobs,' he admitted. After Barnsley he had short spells with Scunthorpe United and Doncaster Rovers, before dropping out of the league to finish his playing days with Bentley Victoria.

Since leaving football, Jimmy has been an insurance agent, milkman, security guard, dry dockman and jetty master – the job he does today.

Back in February 2007, the 'Ashton Gate Eight' were reunited, when the Bristol City Supporters Trust arranged a special evening to commemorate the eight's sacrifice in order to ensure the survival of the club. It was the first time that they'd all been together since walking away from Ashton Gate in 1982. 'I was in two minds about going, but it was good to see the lads again,' said Jimmy.

'I enjoyed my time at City and the fans were always very good to me,' summed up Jimmy. 'Considering that City didn't have to splash out a fee, I think they got their money's worth.'

Married to Christine, the couple have two children – Charlotte and James (the fourth generation of James Manns).

Jimmy in his City days.

Jimmy Mann today.

JULIAN MARSHALL

When Julian Marshall signed for City in the summer of 1980, he couldn't have had any possible idea of the dramatic events that lay ahead. 'I signed for Alan Dicks the season after the club had been relegated from the old First Division,' said Julian. 'I was hoping to play a part in helping them get back into the top flight, instead the club carried on free falling on and off the pitch and I became one of the 'Ashton Gate Eight'.'

A member of the Swansea Schoolboys side, Julian's career began at Leeds United. He moved on to Hereford, managed in those days by former City man John Sillett, with Terry Paine as John's number two. 'I was at Hereford for five years and played around a hundred games for them,' said Julian.

A central defender, on arrival at City Julian found it hard to dislodge the central defensive partnership of David Rodgers and Geoff Merrick, making his debut for City in November 1980 when Merrick was out injured. 'We beat Blackburn two-nil at Ashton Gate and I kept my place for practically the rest of the season,' he pointed out.

Sadly, dreams of restoring past glories with a return to the top flight were never to be for Julian and his team mates, as the side finished second from bottom (neighbours Bristol Rovers were the only side below them) and they crashed into the old Third Division.

It got worse. Julian added a mere four appearances to the 34 games he'd played the previous year, while the side continued on its downward descent. And not only was it a disaster in terms of results, but, come the turn of the year, the club itself was in very real danger of extinction.

'It was a surreal and weird situation when the club decided the only way to survive financially was to ask the senior players to tear up their contracts,' said Julian. 'I felt sorry for the others, they'd been at the club much longer than me, some since their school days.

'After City I signed for Blackburn. The manager there was very straight with me and told me he wanted me as cover for their regular centre backs, which was fair enough. After Blackburn, Julian moved on to Walsall, but spent less than a season there. 'It simply didn't work out for me there,' he summed up.

Out of contract, Julian decided that he'd had enough of full-time soccer, set up his own financial services business and played part-time for Worcester City. 'The trouble was I'd lost a bit of that desire that you need as a footballer and once you've played at a higher level, part-time just isn't the same – not for me anyway,' he admitted.

Married to Claire, who Julian says is a Manchester United season ticket holder, the couple live in a little village in Worcestershire. 'It's an idyllic setting,' said Julian. 'We're surrounded by fields and away from all the hustle and bustle.' They have three children, Jonathon, who is at university, Amy who is at college and Kate, who is still at school.

Julian during his playing days.

Julian Marshall today.

HUGH McILMOYLE

As a professional footballer you know when you've done alright at your club. It's the little things, like having a street named after you and a statue erected in your honour! And that's exactly what happened to Hugh McIlmoyle, whose contribution during three spells with Carlisle United resulted in the street naming and statue erecting. And let's not forget that Hugh also played for Bristol City.

Scotsman Hugh began working life as a ship's painter, before being spotted by a Leicester City scout, while playing for Port Glasgow Rangers. He scored on his debut, the first of many goals, and within eight months, was playing against Spurs in the FA Cup Final.

'A terrific experience, even though we lost,' recalled Hugh. 'It was only my seventh senior game and first ever cup match. It was a boyhood dream, the only real chance you got to play at Wembley in those days, unless you were an international.'

After a couple of seasons with Leicester, Hugh was transferred to Rotherham United, but didn't settle. Then came the start of his 'love affair' with Carlisle United – Hugh joining them in January '63. 'I knew I'd be happy there, the minute I arrived,' he said.

The trouble with being a success at a small club – and with 44 goals in his first season, Hugh was certainly that – is the 'big' clubs come in, waving unrefuseable cheques. 'I didn't really want to leave Carlisle,' admitted Hugh. 'But it was a step up to the (old) First Division and Carlisle simply couldn't turn down the money Wolves were prepared to pay for me.'

But Wolves were no longer the top side that they used to be and despite Hugh averaging a goal every three games, they were relegated. 'I had the best part of three seasons at Molineux, before Bristol City came in for me,' said Hugh.

Hugh got off to flyer with City, scoring on his debut in a 2-1 home win over Hull City. 'There was a good camaraderie at the club, but although I played alongside some good players, like Jantzen Derrick, Chris Crowe and Johnny Quigley, the team struggled.'

With City still struggling at the start of the next season, manager Fred Ford was dismissed. 'Fred was a good man, very straight,' said Hugh. 'After he was sacked, he told me that if I got the chance to move, to take it.'

But, when that chance came, it was back to the club he really wanted to be with – Carlisle. 'Although it meant a wage drop, it was a dream move for me – I was going 'home'. I was even made captain, which I regarded as a great honour.'

Once again though, a big money offer saw Hugh leave Carlisle for Middlesbrough. 'I didn't really want to go, but back then you didn't have much choice. Boro were very good, letting me live and train at Carlisle for part of the week, but the travelling got me down.'

After two years commuting, Hugh was transferred to Preston, and two seasons later joined Scottish club Morton. And when his beloved Carlisle reached the top flight for the first time, they sent for Hugh once again.

At the end of that historic season for Carlisle, the club was relegated and Hugh decided to call it a day. After football, he returned to Leicester, working as a warehouseman for Walkers Crisps, before taking early retirement and moving back to Carlisle.

Married to Rosalyne, the couple have five children and three grandchildren.

A playing days photograph of Hugh.

Hugh outside his Carlisle home.

MICKY MELLON

'It was like a fairy tale. I was a young lad playing amateur football in Scotland and in a matter of months I was on the subs' bench at Ashton Gate for a cup match against Chelsea.' So recalled former Bristol City midfielder Micky Mellon.

Born in Paisley, Micky was spotted at the age of 17, playing for Highland League club Pollock United by City's scouts. 'It was my first move away from Scotland, but I had no problem moving down south,' he said. 'I found City to be a great family club and soon settled in.'

Having made his debut as a substitute in a home match with Wigan, Micky went on to make eight senior starts in his first season, the season City won promotion to the (old) Second Division. 'To be part of a promotion team in my first season was brilliant – a real bonus,' he admitted.

'It was a fantastic growing-up period for me and it stood me in good stead for the future,' pointed out Micky. 'There were some very good players at the club and the older pros, like Gary Shelton, Andy Llewellyn, Mark Gavin and Mark Aizlewood, looked after me.'

Originally signed by Scottish footballing legend Joe Jordan, Micky went on to play for Jimmy Lumsden, Denis Smith and Russell Osman during his four years with City. But, by November '93, his wholehearted displays in City's midfield had attracted the attention of West Bromwich Albion and a fee of £75,000 took him to The Hawthorns.

'There had been talk of clubs being interested in me, but that's par for the course in football if you're playing well,' said Micky. 'But when I was told that a massive club like West Brom wanted me, I couldn't really turn the move down.'

Just as with City, Micky found himself celebrating promotion in his first season with 'The Baggies', going up to the (old) First Division following Play Off Final success. He made around 50 senior starts for the Midlands club, before Sam Allardyce, manager of Blackpool at the time, brought him to Bloomfield Road.

'I had the best part of four seasons there and really enjoyed it,' said Micky.

In October '97, Micky was off on his travels again, another famous name in the soccer world, John Aldridge, splashing out a big fee to bring him to Tranmere Rovers. 'Looking back, I've played for some cracking managers who have played the game at the top level,' mused Micky.

In August 1999, Micky was heading for Lancashire, with Burnley signing the much-in-demand Scot. Yet again, he was to experience the joy of promotion, with the Turf Moor club moving up to the First Division.

Two years on and it was back to Tranmere, where Micky was to enjoy four more seasons, before finishing his league career with Kidderminster Harriers, managed by Jan Molby.

'I got a bad injury at Kidderminster – did my Achilles tendon – and it proved to be one injury too many,' he admitted.

A short spell with non league Witton Albion followed, before Micky hung up his boots. He went on to take up a coaching role with Burnley, before becoming manager of Conference North side Fleetwood Town last September, leading them on a headline grabbing cup run.

Married to Jane, the couple live in Blackpool, where Micky runs a gymnasium. The couple have three sons and two daughters.

Micky during his playing days.

Starting out in football management: Micky Mellon today.

STEVE NEVILLE

When former City striker Steve Neville decided to leave the Football League, his world turned upside down – quite literally. For, after over 15 seasons plying his trade with Southampton, Exeter City (three spells), Sheffield United and, of course, Bristol City, Steve headed to the other side of the globe, first to Hong Kong and then Perth in Western Australia.

Long before Steve was settling down to beach barbies and ice-cold lager, he started off his playing days with Southampton. 'I was spotted by their scouts playing in East London,' said Walthamstow-born Steve, who went on to make his debut at 16. 'It was against Millwall and I was on the right wing. My two striking partners were Mike Channon and Peter Osgood, so they obviously stood out.'

In 1978 Steve moved to the South West, signing for Third Division Exeter City. In his three years there he made over 100 senior appearances, before a transfer to Sheffield United in October 1980. But, with first team opportunities limited, Steve returned to Exeter two years later. In November '84, Steve arrived at Ashton Gate, his good friend Trevor Morgan moving to 'The Grecians' as part of the deal.

'Without doubt, that was the best period of my playing career,' said Steve. 'We had a great bunch of lads who got on well on and off the pitch. Terry [Cooper] was by far the best manager I played under. His man-management and motivational skills were quality. The spirit in the dressing room was superb and that was down to him.'

So, looking back over his 165 games and 49 goals in City's colours, what are his best memories of his time in Bristol? 'A forty-yard chip over Jon Burridge in the Sheffield United goal is one that stands out, and the goal I got in the last minute of extra time against Hereford to take us to Wembley for the Freight Rover Final. I'd been there twice before, with Southampton for the '76 Cup Final and the Charity Shield match, but didn't play in either. Actually playing there is obviously different. The atmosphere as you walk out, the huge crowd...I just kept trying to tell myself that I wasn't nervous.'

A broken leg put the brakes on Steve's City career and, in 1988, he linked up for the third and final time with Exeter City. 'In all honesty, I only went back there because Terry [Cooper] was the manager.'

Having missed out on promotion with City, Steve was an ever present in the Exeter side that won the Fourth Division championship at the end of the 89/90 season. He was to stay one more season with Exeter, before trying his luck in the Far East, playing alongside team mate Trevor Morgan in Hong Kong and South China.

'I loved Hong Kong,' said Steve. 'It's a very different culture and the way we were treated was first class.'

Steve moved on to Australia, initially to help Trevor Morgan coaching Sorrento FC in the Western Australia State League. 'I've been with the club ten years now. When Trevor left, I took over as first team coach.'

Married to Wendy, Steve combines football coaching with his job as a plasterer, alongside son Scott. Bristol-born daughter Danielle is a teacher.

Steve (left) in action for Exeter, alongside team mate and fellow ex Robin Lee Rogers.

Steve, pictured with wife Wendy.

KEVIN NUGENT

Many former Bristol City players have travelled extensively during their soccer careers. From Scotland to the Far East, there aren't many parts of the world they haven't been between them. Former City striker Kevin Nugent knows all about 'the Orient.' In fact, he's been there three times during his career, in fact, he's still there. Not that he needed malaria injections or a passport for the Orient he went to – Leyton Orient.

'Yes, you could say that I've seen a lot of the Orient,' laughed Kevin, who is assistant manager at the club.

Born in Edmonton, London, Kevin joined Leyton Orient from school in 1985. He made his debut in 1987, going on to make over 100 senior appearances for 'The O's' and netting over 20 goals, before moving to Plymouth Argyle in March 1992 for £200,000.

During his three years at Home Park, Kevin added another thirty-plus goals to his cv, clocking up in excess of 150 games. City manager Joe Jordan, no slouch at centre forward himself, recognised Kevin's value to the front line and brought him to Ashton Gate in September 1995, paying Argyle £75,000 for his services.

'Joe was fantastic to work with,' recalled Kevin. 'Having been a centre forward himself, he taught me a great deal.' During his time with The Robins, Kevin played alongside the likes of Paul Agostino and Shaun Goater. 'They were both very good forwards and it was a pleasure to play alongside them,' he added.

'I have some very good memories of my time at Bristol City, particularly the derby matches.'

After around seventy-odd appearances for City and 14 league goals, Kevin went over the bridge to join Cardiff City, totting up 99 appearances and 29 goals in his four-and-a-half years at Ninian Park. Then it was back to square one, as Kevin rejoined Leyton Orient in January 2002. His stay there lasted just a year, before he moved to Swansea City on loan in January 2003, a move made permanent the following month. He went on to play over 70 games for 'The Swans', adding 16 goals to his tally, and had a spell as the club's assistant manager. He subsequently moved back to Leyton Orient, where he was youth team manager, caretaker manager for a short spell and now assistant manager under former Bristol Rovers player Geraint Williams.

'During my career of just under five hundred senior games, I've averaged a goal every four matches, which is a pretty fair ratio for a striker,' he pointed out.

'Looking back, I had a lot of support over the years from my parents and brothers, while Orient coach Patsy Holland was another major influence,' he said.' I have been very fortunate in playing for the biggest clubs outside of the Championship in the south,' said Kevin. 'I enjoyed my time at City and still have friends in the area. I really hope they continue to do well.'

Kevin in action for City.

A more recent photograph of Kevin, taking a
training session.

GARY OWERS

'There's more to life than football, but football will always be part of my life.' So summed up Gary Owers, who notched up close on 600 league appearances in a career that took in Sunderland, Notts County and, of course, Bristol City.

'I became an apprentice at Sunderland at sixteen and went on to make my debut two years later at Brentford,' said Gary. From that debut, given to him incidentally by Denis Smith, who went on to manage City, Gary was to make over 300 appearances for 'The Mackems', including one season in the top flight and also an FA Cup final appearance at Wembley.

'That was a great occasion for the club and the supporters, even though we lost (to Liverpool),' recalled Gary. 'When you think that the great George Best never got to play in an FA Cup final…'

Another of life's ironies was that the last of Gary's many games for Sunderland was actually playing against City.

Two days before Christmas 1994, Gary moved south to sign for Joe Jordan's City side for a fee of £250,000. Anxious to preserve their First Division (now Championship) status, Jordan had plumped for Gary's skill and experience to help turn things around. Sadly, despite some sterling performances by Gary, the club went down. Two years later, with Gary an ever present in City's line up, City finished fifth, but lost out in the Play Offs. It was third time lucky when, under John Ward, the team got promoted.

'I enjoyed playing for Joe and later John Ward, who is probably the best coach I've played under,' commented Gary.

Gary was to spend nearly four years at Ashton Gate, notching up over 150 games and scoring 12 goals for The Robins, playing alongside Shaun Taylor, later to become his number two at Forest Green.

In July '98 Gary packed his bags and moved on to Notts County. Yet another of those soccer ironies that link Gary and Bristol City is that son Joshua was born on the day that Gary played for Notts County….against Bristol City.

Gary was to spend four seasons and play nearly 200 senior games for County, before winding up his league career. 'You know when you get past thirty-four that your playing days in the league are numbered,' he said philosophically.

After a season playing for Forest Green Rovers, Gary took on the role of player-manager at Bath City, where, over three seasons, he did well. His success prompted Forest Green to offer him the manager's job with them, with former team mate Shaun Taylor joining him as assistant. In his first season in charge he took the team to nineteenth in the Conference, but a poor start to the 2006/7 season, saw a parting of the ways.

'It's not a nice experience, getting the bullet, but that's the nature of the beast,' said Gary. 'We had fourteen months at Forest Green and achieved what we were asked to. The truth is managers are simply not given enough time.'

After Rovers, Gary put his boots on to help out Weston-super-Mare Football Club, acting as caretaker player-manager there for a short period.

'These days I get more time to improve my golf,' said Gary. 'I even took a holiday during the season, something I've never done before.'

Married to Karen, the couple live in Chipping Sodbury and have two young sons, Jacob and Joshua.

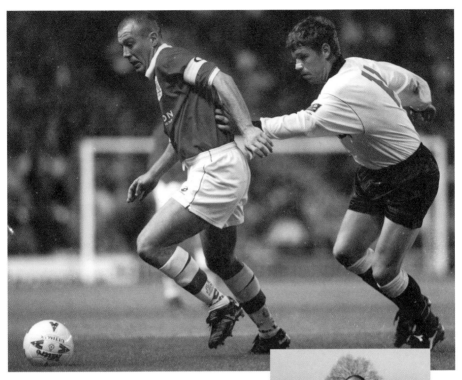

Gary in action for City.

Less of a handicap than soccer management, Gary catches up on his golf.

GLENN PENNYFATHER

Years ago, quite a number clubs had one or two part-timers on their books. As time went on they became fewer and far between, but one man who continued the trend in the eighties and nineties was former Bristol City midfield player Glenn Pennyfather. Not that any of his other clubs needed to worry about his maintaining his fitness levels, for Glenn combined playing professional soccer with the job of PE teacher.

'I've been a school teacher taking physical education since I was twenty-one,' said Glenn, in between taking classes at Crowstone Prep School in Southend. 'I would go to work as a footballer in the mornings and then take PE lessons in the afternoons.'

Born in Billericay in Essex, Glenn joined Southend United, making his first team debut as a 17 year old in 1980. Promoted to the old Third Division in his first season, Glenn began to establish himself in the side the following year and went on to enjoy over 250 games for 'The Shrimpers'.

A firm favourite with the fans as a hard-tackling midfielder, Glenn was soon attracting attention from the bigger clubs. An offer from Crystal Palace, then managed by Steve Coppell, saw Glenn depart from Roots Hall. 'It was a wrench to leave, but that's the nature of the job and it meant moving up a division to a club chasing promotion to the top flight,' he explained. 'Another plus was linking up with players like Mark Bright, John Salako and Ian Wright.'

Although the side went on to win promotion, Glenn's appearances were restricted by injuries, including cracked ribs, chipped bones and ruptured knee ligaments. 'I missed about seven months, so when I was fit again I was happy to move on to Ipswich Town, as it was not far from my home.'

Here again, the injury hoodoo struck. 'I had knee ligament problems soon after making my debut and by the time I was fully fit again, John Duncan, who had signed me, had gone and the new manager was assembling his own team,' he pointed out.

A chance to go to Bristol City on loan in early '93 was snapped up by Glenn and he soon settled into The Robins midfield. 'It's a massive club and I loved it at Bristol,' he said. 'It was great to be playing first-team football again and the fans were brilliant towards me.

'They had some useful players there – Gary Shelton, Junior Bent, Andy Llewellyn and, of course, Jackie Dziekanowski and Andy Cole.'

After his initial loan spell, Glenn's move was made permanent and he went on to make around 30 appearances for the side. 'Then I got a bad knock at Birmingham and ended up having two operations for chipped bones. I realised it was one injury too many to carry on playing professional football,' he confessed.

Moving into non-league football, Glenn made his mark with Canvey Island, a side that enjoyed a phenomenal climb up the non-league pyramid. 'Jeff King, the manager, got me involved in the coaching side and over ten years we gained four promotions, reaching the Conference. When Jeff moved on for a new challenge with Chelmsford City in the Ryman Premier League, I went with him as his number two,' said Glenn.

Glenn lives in Billericay. He has two sons and a daughter from his previous marriage.

Glenn during his playing days.
(photo: Peter Hurn)

Physical education teacher and assistant
football manager Glenn Pennyfather.
(photo: Matt Bradshaw)

FORBES PHILLIPSON-MASTERS

You don't have to be a genius to work out that the player with the longest surname in Bristol City's history is Forbes Phillipson-Masters, a commanding centre half who joined The Robins back in the eighties from Plymouth Argyle.

'I probably had the longest surname in the whole league,' laughed Forbes. 'Mind you, I still had my fair share of bookings, so that didn't deter referees from getting their pencils and notebooks out!'

Forbes actually started out as a goalkeeper. 'I signed for Southampton as a schoolboy, having played goalie for a local junior side. The club decided I wasn't going to make it between the sticks, but manager Lawrie McMenemy and the coach, John McGrath, who had been a central defender, saw something in me that convinced them that, with the right training, I could make a go of it in defence,' he explained.

Signing as a pro for 'The Saints' in 1974, Forbes went on to make a number of appearances for them, including the Anglo-Italian Cup Winners Final in Naples. He also enjoyed loan spells with Exeter, Bournemouth and Luton Town, before moving to Plymouth Argyle in 1979.

'I signed for City in November 1982, with the club looking to stabilise after relegation and the financial problems it had been through,' said Forbes. 'There were some good players at the club. Tom Ritchie, who was class, had come back, Rob Newman, who you could see would go on to bigger things and John Shaw, who was a cracking keeper.'

After finishing around mid-table in the (old) Fourth Division, the club achieved promotion in Forbes's second season. 'There was an excellent team spirit and the side knitted well together. In Terry Cooper, the club had a first-rate manager and our promotion was thoroughly deserved. Also, it was great to do it for the fans, who gave us terrific support, despite the hard times they'd had to endure.'

Talking of the fans, there was a story about Forbes that has probably entered soccer folklore. At one game, so the story goes, the fans were chanting out Forbes surname, letter by letter. You know the sort of thing. 'Give us a P..PP..give us an H..HH..' and so on. When they finished chanting 'give us an N..NN' at the end of Phillipson, the next chant was 'give us a hyphen..hyphen hyphen!!' 'I can't say I remember that,' said Forbes, with a laugh, 'but it would have been typical of some of the terrace humour!'

Virtually an ever present during the promotion season, Forbes played 31 games the following season, before signing for (then) non-league Yeovil Town in the summer of 1986.

'I was having problems with my Achilles tendon and stepped down from full-time to sign for Gerry Gow at Yeovil,' explained Forbes. 'Also, I'd started up a painting and decorating business, but later found playing for Yeovil, plus the travelling, was getting too much.'

After leaving Yeovil, Forbes moved to Verwood in Dorset and for a number of years, managed the Dorset County Football Association's senior representative side. He has expanded his business and is involved in building and development.

'I enjoyed my time at City and still look out for their results,' said Forbes.

Married to Lynne, the couple have two sons, James and Oliver.

Clean-up time after another City win,
Forbes is top left.

A more recent photograph of Forbes.

DICKIE ROOKS

Centre half Dickie Rooks was such a firm favourite with the fans at Middlesbrough that he won their Player of the Year award twice. But, when he fell out with Boro boss Stan Anderson, City wasted no time in bringing him to Ashton Gate as a successor to the popular long-serving defender Jack Connor. He went on to complete over 100 games for the club.

'I'd had some good years at Boro, but Stan dropped me two games from the end of the season and didn't have the bottle to tell me face to face. I had been an ever present and thought he handled it badly. I knew I could never play for him again,' said Dickie.

On Sunderland's books as a schoolboy, Dickie learnt a trade as a carpenter and joiner before going full time. He made his senior debut at 18, but, with Charlie Hurley a fixture in the side and first-team opportunities limited, he moved to Boro in August '65, the last signing made by the legendary Raich Carter. In the summer of '69, after his falling out with Carter's successor and, with 136 League appearances for the club behind him, Dickie headed for Bristol.

'My wife and I went down to discuss the move with City. They offered treble what I was on at Boro, plus a new house in Stockwood, but it was never about money,' said Dickie.

Dickie was soon established in the side, going on to skipper the team. 'There were some good players at the club. Chris Garland was making his mark, Trevor Tainton and Gerry Gow were coming through, John Galley was a good centre forward and there was Alan Skirton on the wing. For such a big guy he could move.'

But an injury at Leicester was to spell the beginning of the end for Dickie's playing days. 'It was pouring with rain and I went in for a tackle and couldn't stop,' recalled Dickie. 'As I collided with the other player, I knew it was serious.' Dickie battled on, but realises now that, if the injury had been properly diagnosed and treated, his career could have been saved. 'It should have been x-rayed straight away, but wasn't. I continued to play on, without knowing that I'd cracked a bone in my knee, which had splintered. Everytime I jumped for a ball, the pain was excruciating when I landed.'

Eventually Dickie underwent an exploratory operation. 'I tried to keep playing, but the knee would keep flaring up. I'd often have to skip training just so I could play on the Saturday, but the following morning the knee would balloon up again. I couldn't carry on and was advised to quit, so I returned to Sunderland and my original trade as a carpenter and opened a DIY shop.'

But Dickie was tempted back into football, taking up the manager's post at Scunthorpe United. 'I should never have taken the job,' he admitted. After nearly two years there, Dickie tried his luck overseas, coaching in Tanzania. 'That was OK until the war with Uganda broke out and we had to leave.'

Back home Dickie coached for the FA and also the Sunderland School of Excellence, but gave up football altogether when diagnosed with diabetes. Married to Doris, the couple, who have three sons, live in Tyne & Wear.

Dickie in action in his City days.

A more recent photograph of City's
former centre half.
(photo: www.shaunkeogh.co.uk)

JOE ROYLE

Every footballer wants to make a good impression when he signs for a new club, especially if he's been brought in to solve their goal scoring problem. So, netting four goals on your Bristol City debut is not a bad way to start. 'The only problem was, I didn't get another one for the next ten games!' laughed Joe Royle.

Arriving to replace the injured Paul Cheesley, Joe couldn't have imagined his first game would go so well, as a crowd of 21,000 thought that Christmas had come early that November day in 1977. 'It was the stuff that dreams are made off,' said Joe, with only visiting Middlesbrough and their travelling fans regretting his arrival. 'I remember in the bath afterwards, one of the lads turning to me to say "that makes you the club's top scorer!" Of course, it became a millstone round my neck. I mean, you can't go around scoring four goals every week!'

Joe had arrived at City with an impressive cv, having made a name for himself at Everton and Manchester City and winning six England caps along the way. 'I made my debut for Everton in 1966 when I was sixteen – the youngest player to start a first team game for them,' pointed out Joe. He went on to clock up nearly 300 games for 'The Toffees,' scoring 119 goals and was top scorer for five seasons. Manchester City paid £170,000 to take him to Maine Road in December 1974. Three years there saw him add over 100 senior appearances to his portfolio, before he answered Alan Dicks' SOS to help lift Bristol City out of the top-flight relegation zone.

'I came down initially on loan, but fell in love with the club and the area,' said Joe. 'We got a place in Wrington, it's probably the nicest home we've had on my travels.'

City had paid £90,000 to make Joe's move permanent and he went on to play his part in City avoiding relegation that season. The following year he helped them achieve a mid-table position, scoring another eight goals to match the eight he'd got the previous season. But his value to the team wasn't just his goals. It was also his experience and his ability to set up chances for the likes of Tom Ritchie and emerging star Kevin Mabbutt. 'There were a great bunch of lads at Ashton Gate – Gerry Sweeney, Geoff Merrick, Norman Hunter, Chris Garland…I still keep in touch with many of them.'

Joe's third season at City saw the club struggle and they were relegated. Joe, having notched up 120 appearances and 21 goals, departed for Norwich City for a season and a bit, before succumbing to a niggling knee injury and hanging up his boots.

But, as we know, Joe was also to make his mark as a manager, enjoying success at Oldham, Everton, Man City and Ipswich. Ironically, he nearly began his management career with Bristol City. 'I came down for an interview for the manager's position, but it went to Terry [Cooper] instead. But that's football and Terry did a very good job at City.'

'Looking back, I think that Bristol City getting into the old First Division was one of the great feats of modern soccer history and I really enjoyed being part of their last three seasons in the top flight.'

Married to Janet, the couple have three sons and live near Southport.

Joe in action for Everton.

A recent reunion with old team mate
Chris Garland.

RAY SAVINO

Back in the fifties and early sixties, wingers were crucial to a side's success. Every team had them, one on either flank. They were usually the shortest members of the forward line, generally weren't renowned for scoring lots of goals, but their job description did require them to take on their full back, get to the byline and put in some decent crosses so that one of their fellow forwards could grab the limelight by putting the ball into the back of the net. One such winger was Ray Savino, a swarthy-looking individual, who came to Ashton Gate in the summer of 1962.

Born in Norwich, Ray ('Savvy' to fans and team mates) inherited his Mediterranean looks from his father, who was half Italian. He joined the Norwich City groundstaff at 16, having been spotted playing as a goalscoring inside forward for a local boys' team. A sheet metal worker when he left school, Ray was to spend six years on the books at Carrow Road. It was during a game for Norwich reserves at Eastville that Ray came to the attention of Bristol City. 'I think City's manager Fred Ford watched that match and I recall having a decent game, which prompted his interest,' explained Ray.

After negotiations for his transfer had reached an advanced stage, City manager Ford met Ray at Temple Meads and took him for a T-bone steak as they finalised the move. 'I remember Fred telling me to enjoy the steak – it would be the last one I'd get from the club!'

Ray duly signed on the dotted line in that summer of 1962 and lived in a club house with Jantzen Derrick, Mike Thresher and Bobby Etheridge as neighbours. 'In those days they had club houses to put the players up in. Those days are long gone – in fact, most footballers in the top division could probably buy a street of houses!'

For the next two seasons the pint-sized winger was in and out of the side, vying with Jantzen Derrick, Roger Peters and Alex Tait for the number seven shirt. It was during the successful 64/65 promotion season that he made the shirt his own, making 38 senior appearances. Ironically, given it was City's promotion season and Ray had established himself as a regular in the side, a bad injury towards the end of the campaign was to prove disastrous for the popular forward.

'We were playing up at Carlisle in April,' recalled Ray. 'With both of us chasing promotion it was a very important game. I got a bad knock, but as there were no substitutes in those days, I limped on, rather than leave us a man short. Of course, it wouldn't happen today, with umpteen subs on the bench. Later it turned out that I'd fractured my leg and staying on was hardly ideal in terms of dealing with the injury.'

Although Ray was to spend two more seasons at City, he would probably admit that he was never the same player again and made just another 11 senior appearances, bringing his total of City games to 80, before he left Ashton Gate and headed back home to Norfolk. There he joined non-league King's Lynn, playing for them for four years and working as a brick layer.

Now retired, Ray lives with wife Carol in Norwich. They have a daughter, Sonia.

Ray in his Bristol City days.

Ray Savino today.

MARTIN SCOTT

Over the years City have had some excellent left backs. There was Mike Thresher, Alec Briggs, 'Chippy' Drysdale, Geoff Merrick and Terry Cooper. In more recent times came Darren Barnard and Mickey Bell. And no list of outstanding City left backs would be complete without Yorkshireman Martin Scott.

Martin arrived at Ashton Gate in December 1990, via Rotherham United, where he had clocked up nearly 100 appearances. The fee was £200,000 – a bargain, given the 200 senior games he would play for The Robins and that the club would nearly quadruple their money when he moved on.

Originally a midfield player, Martin found himself switched to left back when Rotherham had an injury crisis. He excelled in his new position and just before Christmas 1990, Bristol City agreed a fee to bring him to Ashton Gate.

Three days after signing, Martin made his debut, a home fixture against Sheffield Wednesday. But plans to return to Yorkshire after the game went out the window, thanks to the weather. 'It started snowing during the game and, by the time it was all over, we were snowed in,' he revealed. And not just Martin. 'My mum and dad had come down to watch me, so they were stranded too.' Martin's problem was solved when City's chairman put them all up.

Over the next four years Martin's was to be an automatic name on the team sheet. He also took on the role of the side's penalty-taker – odd, given the fact that he'd never taken one before. 'I think the team had missed a few just before I joined and when we were awarded one soon after I arrived, no one seemed keen, so I took it.' And, during the course of his 200 City games, Martin was to find the back of the net 16 times, many of those goals coming from the penalty spot.

A winner of the coveted Player of the Year award during his four-and-a-half seasons at Ashton Gate, it was inevitable that his consistent performances would attract the attention of other clubs. And, in December '94, Martin was heading for Sunderland in a £750,000 deal.

Martin was to play a key role in Sunderland's winning the League One championship, only for the team to go straight back down again. The 97/98 season saw them lose out in the Play Offs, before winning promotion back to the top tier the year after. But a nasty injury in a cup match at Lincoln put the dampeners on the celebrations.

'I knew it was bad immediately,' recalled Martin. 'My leg was broken and I also needed reconstruction surgery on my ankle.'

By the time Martin was anywhere near fit again, his contract at the club was up. 'I had an offer to join Bradford City in The Premiership,' said Martin. 'They knew all about my injuries, but I passed the medical and signed a three-year deal. Unfortunately, I broke down in pre-season training and knew it was all over.'

Anxious to continue in the game, Martin went to help out at Hartlepool United. He progressed through the ranks, becoming manager in May 2005. 'I was manager for just seven months and took the team to the League One Play Off Finals.'

After Hartlepool, Martin had a season as assistant manager at Bury, before joining the coaching staff at Middlesbrough, where he is reserve team manager.

Martin in playing days action.
(photo: Sunderland FC)

After playing, it was management and
coaching for Martin.
(photo: Hartlepool United FC)

GERRY SHARPE

A goalscoring first team regular, Gerry Sharpe had to go through the trauma of seeing his footballing days brought to a premature end while in his prime. No one who was at Ashton Gate that day in 1971 will ever forget the sight of Gerry lying in agony on the pitch, his leg so badly broken that players from both sides turned away in horror. As Gerry was taken off by stretcher and rushed to hospital, many feared the worse.

In and out of a hospital for a year, Gerry battled gamely for two years to get back into the game. 'I played about a dozen reserve matches and scored eight or nine goals, but I would get problems with the leg straight afterwards and in the end I had to accept the inevitable,' said Gerry.

Gerry's short but distinguished career with The Robins began when he was spotted playing in the Gloucester junior league. Under the management of Fred Ford, he progressed through the ranks, before making his first-team debut in the autumn of 1964. He went on to net six goals in his 16 first-team appearances that season, culminating in the final game of the season, when City beat Oldham two-nil in front of a packed Ashton Gate, to win promotion to the (old) Second Division. 'That game stands out as one of my best City memories,' recalled Gerry.

Over the next three seasons Gerry featured in over 50 senior appearances, but it was in the 1968/69 season that manager Alan Dicks switched Gerry to outside left and he revelled in his new role. By the time the ill-fated home match with Middlesbrough came around, on 16th January '71, Gerry had clocked up nearly 180 games, scored 54 goals and was a first-team regular.

'For a long time after I'd finished playing, I couldn't face going to the ground,' he admitted. But Gerry did go back, taking up a role as youth team coach. He even got a run as caretaker manager, losing just one game during his six-match manager's stint.

During his time as youth coach Gerry had taken the opportunity to see what was happening in The States, accepting an invitation to see first-hand the soccer revolution happening there and so, in 1985, he packed his bags to take up a post as director of soccer. 'I had six years with Richmond Strikers, coaching youngsters at grass roots level and found it very rewarding,' he said.

After Richmond, Gerry moved on to become director of soccer with Beach FC in Virginia, playing a key role in the growth of soccer in the area. 'The Virginia Beach area is very similar in size to Bristol, although the climate is more like the south of France than the south of Bristol!' he said with a laugh.

As well as finding his niche in the USA, Gerry also found his future wife Patti, a Virginia Beach girl he met in 1990. He has a son and daughter from his first marriage and is immensely proud of both them. 'Robert works for the BBC, while Julie is a remedial therapist in Australia,' he said.

'Coming to The States was an opportunity too good to miss,' summed up Gerry. 'Mind you, I still miss Cornish pasties, the odd pint of beer and English fish and chips!'

Spot the ball! Gerry (11) and Chris Garland are
thwarted by the Derby defence.

Gerry today, at Beach FC's new training centre.

GEORGE SHOWELL

Different generations remember their glory teams. Looking back at the top flight over the second half of the last century, there was the double-winning Spurs side of the early sixties. We had 'dirty' Leeds, 'boring' Arsenal and Cloughies Forest in the seventies; the glorious Liverpool side of the eighties and love 'em or hate 'em, Fergie's Man United dominating the nineties. But let's go right back to the fifties. A time when, under the leadership of the legendary Stan Cullis, Wolverhampton Wanderers were the driving force. Defender George Showell was part of the Cullis success for all of that decade, before coming to the South West and Bristol City.

'Stan Cullis – he should have got a knighthood for what he achieved,' said George. 'Under him, Wolves were three times League champions, finished runners-up three times and third twice and twice won the FA Cup. 'In fact,' went on George, 'when we won the FA Cup at the end of the 59/60 season, we missed the League championship by one point.'

George, now in his seventies, signed up with Wolves as a 17-year-old in 1951. 'I was originally an amateur and signed up the same day as another young lad – Ron Flowers,' he recalled. In and out of the side in the early days, George was a regular by 1959 and went on to play in their cup final win over Blackburn Rovers. 'Winning the cup at Wembley with Wolves – a fantastic memory,' he said with a smile.

Sadly, in football, nothing stays the same and when Cullis was axed in 1964, George could have been forgiven for thinking it was time to move on, after well over 200 games in Wolves' gold and black.

Bristol City, who had just come up from the (old) Third Division, were looking to strengthen their side and manager Fred Ford was well aware of George's capabilities.

'I'd been at Wolves so long that I was a bit dubious about the move, but Fred convinced me and I went on to enjoy my time in Bristol,' said George.

So, which players stand out from his time at Ashton Gate? 'Jack Connor and Gordon Low were pretty solid in defence, Janzen Derrick was a very skilful player and, of course, there was 'Big John' Atyeo,' he replied.

A knee injury, plus the consistency of full backs Tony Ford and Alec Briggs, restricted George's appearances in City's team, although he has the distinction of being the club's first-ever substitute, coming on for the injured John Atyeo at Maine Road.

After a year and a dozen or so appearances for City, George moved on to Fourth Division Wrexham, where he went on to play for another couple of seasons, before serving the club in a number of capacities, including assistant manager, caretaker manager and physio.

George has also been the physio for the local rugby club, worked as a pharmacy porter at Wrexham Maelor Hospital and done voluntary work for the homeless.

Married to his 'better half' Gwen – they recently celebrated their Golden Wedding Anniversary – the couple have a son, Mark, daughter Tracy and three grandchildren.

It may have been a wrench for George to leave Wolverhampton, but he seems to have taken to living in Wrexham. 'We've been here over forty years now, so I think we've settled in alright!'

FA Cup success for George (standing, far right) and his Wolves team in 1959.

George today.

RONNIE SINCLAIR

It's a bit like home from home for former Bristol players at Stoke City. Not that any of them feature on the playing staff, but the coaching staff – that's a different matter. And one of a number of former City and Rovers players involved behind the scenes is ex-City goalkeeper Ronnie Sinclair.

Born in Scotland, Ronnie was spotted playing for Stirling Boys Club by a Nottingham Forest scout. 'I went to Nottingham for a trial and got myself a contract,' said Ronnie. 'Those were the glory days of Brian Clough and he was the best education I could possibly have had.'

With competition for the keeper's jersey tight – Peter Shilton was the custodian when Ronnie arrived – the young Scot was given the chance to go out on loan. 'I went to Wrexham for a while and played in the Welsh Cup Final, as well as about a dozen league games,' said Ronnie. He was also to have short-term stays at Derby, Sheffield United and Leeds, acting as cover for their regular keepers. 'It was all good experience,' he added.

Leeds United made Ronnie's move a permanent one by signing him on transfer deadline day. But, with Mervyn Day holding down the first-team keeper's job, Ronnie was restricted to a handful of appearances, although he did get league action with another loan move, this time to Halifax Town.

In September '89, Ronnie moved to the South West, signing for Joe Jordan's Bristol City. 'Joe is a legend, which was one of the reasons I signed. Also, there were already a couple of lads there that I knew from my Leeds days – Bob Taylor and Dave Rennie.'

Ronnie settled in quickly and made his senior debut in December in a cup win over Fulham, taking over the keeper's jersey from Andy Leaning. He kept his place in the side, as they went on a great cup run and won promotion from the old Third Division.

'The cup win over Chelsea was a great memory and, although we won promotion, it was as runners up to Rovers. I was in goal when they beat us at Twerton Park and that still sticks in my throat.'

The departure of Jordan saw Jimmy Lumsden take over the managerial reins and he kept faith with Ronnie. But an injury over Christmas saw Ronnie sidelined, with Andy Leaning back between the sticks. And when Lumsden signed a new keeper – Keith Welch – in the summer of 1991, it was time to start packing the suitcase.

A loan spell at Walsall proved to be a good move, as Ronnie played so well in a game against Stoke, that 'The Potters' signed him. At the end of that season, with Ronnie firmly established between the posts, the club narrowly missed promotion from The Third. But the following year they finished top of the table to go up. And, over the course of five years, Ronnie was to play over 100 senior games.

A free transfer took Ronnie to Chester in 1996, where he made some 70 league appearances. At the end of his first season there he was awarded the club's Player of the Year award, after conceding just 43 goals. He was to have one more season at Chester, before returning to Stoke to join the coaching staff.

Ronnie and wife Claire live in The Potteries with their two teenage sons.

Ronnie in his playing days.

Now on the coaching staff at Stoke City.
(photo: *Staffordshire Sentinel News & Media*)

PETER SPIRING

When former Bristol City striker Peter Spiring found himself transferred to the mighty Liverpool and in the presence of Bill Shankly, probably the top manager of the time, it was only natural that he might have felt just a little bit nervous. So when 'Shanks' introduced him to the press as 'the fastest player in the west' he could have been forgiven for feeling he was on a hiding to nothing. 'An introduction like that takes a lot of living up to,' said Peter wryly.

Born in Glastonbury, Peter joined City as a junior in the late sixties. Mindful of the hazards of being a professional footballer, he wisely decided to finish his apprenticeship as an electrician before committing himself to football full time.

'Alan Dicks was the man who gave me my first full-time contract and also my league debut,' recalled Peter. He went on to make seven appearances that season, but the following year was established in the side, notching up 33 appearances and netting 10 goals.

'There was a very good team spirit at the club and some great lads,' said Peter. 'Keith Fear was a very talented player and Geoff Merrick and David Rodgers were solid at the back.'

The following season Peter picked up where he had left off and by Christmas his name was regularly featured in the transfer gossip of local and national newspapers. 'There were rumours that some of the big clubs were after me and then Liverpool came in with an offer of £60,000.'

So, in March 1973, having played over 70 games for City and scored 17 goals, Peter was off to Anfield. But, after Shankly's initial build up, things went downhill. 'I'd been on the subs' bench for the first team, but then got a bad injury in the reserves,' he said. A snapped Achilles tendon meant Peter was out of the game for a long time. 'I thought I was finished at the time and was in plaster for ages,' he pointed out. 'But life and winning games has to go on at clubs like Liverpool and after eighteen months I was sold to Luton Town.'

Luton's manager, the late Harry Haslam, knew a good striker when he saw one – after all, he'd discovered Malcolm MacDonald. But, again, fate in the form of another bad injury, put paid to Peter's Luton career after just 15 games.

'Things weren't going well at Luton when John Sillett, who'd been one of my coaches at City, came in with the chance to start again at Hereford,' said Peter.

After initially signing on loan, Peter joined the club on a permanent basis, helping them win promotion to the (old) Second Division, playing alongside former City team mate John Galley. He went on to make over 250 senior appearances for the club, experiencing the ups and downs of promotion, relegation and re-election, before another bad injury, to his cruciate ligament, proved to be one too many.

These days, Peter lives with his wife June in Hereford. They have a daughter, Elisa, and son Reuben, a former top-class cricketer with Worcestershire. They also have two grandchildren. And the electrical apprenticeship that Peter insisted on completing in his youth, has stood him in good stead – he has his own electrical contracting business.

Peter was a talented footballer who was unlucky with injuries, and fans at The Kop would never know whether Peter really was the fastest player in the west.

Peter in his Bristol City days.

Peter Spiring today.

STEVE STACEY

The first Afro-American footballer in England, Steve Stacey has led an interesting life, which has seen him cope with all the usual racial problems of the time, as he went on to play for City (twice), Wrexham, Ipswich Town, Chester, Charlton and Exeter. Later he moved to Australia.

'My father was a black American soldier stationed in Bristol during the war, while my mum – Evelyn – was a white lady,' explained Steve. Refused permission to marry by the US army, his father returned to America, leaving Steve to be brought up by his mum, grandmother and aunts – no easy task, given public attitudes then.

A gifted footballer, Steve joined Bristol City as a youngster. He went on to score many goals in the youth and reserve teams, but found it hard to break into the first team, although he did score in a rare senior outing in January '62, a 4-2 victory over Merthyr Tydfil in a cup game.

In 1966 Steve agreed to join Fourth Division Wrexham. He spent nearly three years with them, making over 100 senior appearances and was soon drawing scouts from the top flight. In 1968, Ipswich Town paid £25,000 for his transfer.

'Ipswich was not the happy experience it should have been,' admitted Steve. 'The manager who signed me left and it became obvious that I wasn't one of the new manager's favoured players.'

Loan spells at Chester, Northampton and Charlton came to nothing. 'I did score on my debut for Charlton and they wanted me to join the club permanently, but I didn't take to living in London.'

In September 1970, Steve was back where he started, signing for Bristol City and playing in the old Second Division under manager Alan Dicks. For the next two months he was a regular in the side. 'I came back initially on loan and then signed for the season. It was all going well, when I got injured again and was out for another six weeks.'

Anxious to prove his fitness after injury, Steve went in hard on star striker John Galley in a practice match. Too hard for Alan Dicks' liking. 'It was a bit of a crunch tackle, but John was, and still is, a friend. But Alan was livid, words were exchanged and I never played in the first team again.'

And so, in September '71, Steve moved on to Exeter, where he spent two seasons. 'We moved down to Exeter, but then my hamstring went again and then I tore an Achilles tendon twice and was in plaster.' To make matters worse, Steve's wife was taken ill and finished up in hospital in Bristol. 'With all that going on, I wasn't giving the injury time to heal and it was a case of going on with the madness or getting out.'

Steve got a job with a travel firm and played some games for Bath City, while considering his future. And in 1973, he and his family decided to emigrate to Australia. 'We stayed two years, came back, I went to Teacher Training College as a mature student and then we settled in Western Australia.'

Steve still managed to play a decent standard of football down under and has skippered the Western Australia State team. He works for Nyoongar Sports Association as chief executive officer, promoting sport among the local indigenous population in the south west area of Western Australia.

Married to his childhood sweetheart Dot, the couple have two daughters and six grandchildren.

Steve in his Bristol City days.

Enjoying life in Australia: Steve Stacey today.

MIKE STOWELL

Mike Stowell very nearly didn't embark on the long career that saw him play almost 500 league games over a 20 year period. 'I was on Preston's books as a youngster and they offered me a year's full-time contract to act as cover for their regular keeper,' explained Mike. 'The thing was, I had security in the form of an apprenticeship with British Telecom, erecting poles, fixing cables, that sort of thing, so I turned Preston's offer down.'

Fortunately for Mike, Preston manager Alan Kelly, no mean goalkeeper himself in his day, hadn't forgotten the promise Mike had shown and, when he later joined the coaching staff at Everton, he recommended that they sign Mike.

'Everton offered me a two-and-a-half year full-time contract. Now that was too good to turn down,' explained Mike. 'I mean, join the (then) league champions and learn from the best goalie in the business (Neville Southall) or carry on climbing poles for Busby – the BT mascot Busby, not the Man United manager!'

Mike was to spend five years at Everton and although he didn't play a single league game for them, he learnt a lot. 'Neville was the undisputed number one at Everton, a fantastic keeper and Bobby Mimms, another useful goalie, was his deputy,' said Mike. 'I learnt so much training with them and, to get first-team experience, was loaned out to a couple of clubs.'

'A couple of clubs' is a bit of an understatement, as, over the following seasons, he wore the keeper's jersey for Chester City, York City, Manchester City, Port Vale, Wolves and even his first club, Preston.

In 1990, Everton and Wolves agreed a fee of around £275,000 for Mike and he was on his way to Molineux. During his 11 years there he played a record number of games for a Wanderers goalkeeper (447) and also held the record for keeping the most consecutive 'clean sheets'.

Released by the club at the age of 35, Mike had a number of offers to consider. 'Bristol City got in touch. Their senior goalkeeper, Billy Mercer, was trying to recover from injury, leaving just Steve Phillips as the only experienced keeper. Danny Wilson, who I'd played against years before, offered a two-year deal and I came to Bristol.'

Not that everyone shared Danny's enthusiasm about the new signing. 'The club chairman seemed a bit dubious, given the fact that I was thirty-five!' admitted Mike, who got off to a good start with the team winning at Northampton and Mike keeping a 'clean sheet.'

'I had a run in the first team, then I was out for seven weeks with a groin injury.' Once he was fit again, Mike reclaimed his place in the side and, at the same time, was happy to spend time giving specialist coaching to Phillips.

A cartilage operation meant more time on the sidelines and, after undergoing reconstructive surgery on his shoulder, Mike gave up playing (he made 25 league appearances for The Robins) to concentrate on coaching.

In the summer of 2005, having spent four years at City, Mike joined Leicester as goalkeeping coach – the start of a roller-coaster ride with 'The Foxes', which included helping to take charge of the first team, leaving the club, and then returning again.

These days Mike continues to groom the goalkeepers at Leicester, where he lives with his partner Rachel and baby daughter Ella Rose.

Mike in goalkeeping action.

Mike Stowell today.
(photo: Leicester City FC/Raymonds
Press Agency)

ALEX TAIT

Alex Tait began his career with Newcastle United, before coming to the South West to play for City and later settling in the Midlands. 'I was born in West Sleekburn, a tiny mining village in Northumberland, although the pits have long since closed down,' said Alex.

On Newcastle United's books as a junior, Alex was in exalted company at St James' Park, as the star-studded Magpies enjoyed FA Cup success, with a side that were always 'there abouts' when it came to the league championship. 'Those were the days of Jackie Milburn, Joe Harvey, Jimmy Scoular and Ronnie Simpson,' recalled Alex.

During his time with United, Alex made over 30 league appearances. One of the reasons that he didn't play more was undoubtedly because he chose to be a 'part-timer'. 'There was a maximum wage and players weren't particularly well paid,' said Alex. 'I always knew that I needed something else and took my qualifications to be a teacher.'

In the summer of 1960 Alex packed his bags, put school teaching on hold and signed for City. 'The maximum wage had been abolished and I was offered the chance to move to Bristol City,' he said. 'The funny thing was that City were between managers at the time and Les Bardsley was caretaker manager, prior to the appointment of Fred Ford.'

Alex soon settled down in his new surroundings and struck up a good partnership with the legendary Atyeo. 'I lived in the Bedminster area, just a few doors down from my old Newcastle team mate Tom Casey,' said Alex. 'On the pitch John Atyeo was easy to play alongside and we notched up quite a few goals between us. The trouble was we used to let in quite a few as well!'

Those were the days when scores of 5-2 or 4-3 were the norm and it's interesting to note that in Alex's first season at Ashton Gate, City scored four or more goals in no fewer than 11 matches.

Alex was to spend four years with City, but spent the last two commuting from the Midlands, having moved there to help with his father-in-law's 'rag trade' business. Altogether he was to notch up 134 senior games and score 44 goals in City's colours, before departing for a season with Doncaster Rovers. 'I spent a year at Belle Vue, but the travelling was getting me down and you know, as a player, that the clock is ticking.'

After Doncaster, Alex moved to non-league Burton Albion, managed by Peter Taylor. 'I knew Peter from his time as a player with Middlesbrough and he persuaded me to join the club,' explained Alex. 'When he left to start his successful partnership with Brian Clough, he asked me if I would take over at Burton. I wasn't overkeen and turned it down, but he and the chairman asked me to give it a go on a caretaker basis, so I did. I managed them for three years and enjoyed it.'

But, in addition to his time in football, Alex went on to make his mark in the teaching profession, with maths and physical education his prime subjects. He finished his teaching days at Allestree Woodlands Comprehensive in Derbyshire, where he was deputy head, retiring in 1991.

Married to Paula, the couple live in Staffordshire and have two daughters, a son and three grandchildren.

Alex in his City days.

A more recent photograph of Alex Tait.

BOB TAYLOR

Ask any City supporter to name their City 'dream team' and it's fair bet that, if they've been watching them for more than 20 years, one of the first names on their team sheet would be striker Bob Taylor, the first City player to net more than 30 goals in a season since John Atyeo.

It was in the promotion season of 1989/90 that Bob found the back of the net a staggering 34 times, winning the 'Golden Boot' award. This achievement was all the more remarkable when you consider that he missed a number of games through injury. 'You have to remember that any striker is only as good as the service he gets,' said Bob. 'Mark Gavin was a superb crosser of the ball. There was also Robbie Turner alongside me and we formed a great partnership.'

Altogether Bob scored 237 goals in 684 appearances, a goal ratio better than one in three. And yet, Bob became a striker by accident. 'At schoolboy and county level I'd always played full back or centre half,' revealed Bob. 'One day we had a relief teacher for PE and he moved me up front and I just couldn't stop scoring.'

By the age of 17 Bob was playing amateur football for Horden Colliery Welfare. The side was managed by former Sunderland full back Dick Malone and he wasted no time in getting his striker a trial with Leeds United. 'I went to Leeds for a month's trial. I'd never been that far from home in County Durham in my life,' recalled Bob.

The trial went well, with Bob getting a hat trick in his first match for the club's youth team. With a year's contract under his belt, Bob established himself as top scorer in the reserves and by the 1987/88 season had made the first team.

The following season Howard Wilkinson, who had taken over the manager's chair, agreed a deal to sell Bob to Bristol City, taking £240,000 and Carl Shutt in exchange. 'Bob Taylor was a natural goalscorer and this was the prime need of my team,' said Joe Jordan, City's manager at the time.

'It was a fresh challenge for me and I was up for it,' recalled Bob. Having signed for the club towards the end of March, Bob gave a taste of things to come with a return of eight goals from 12 games.

'We had a strong team which included Andy Llewellyn and Glenn Humphries – now there's two guys I wouldn't want to play against.'

And so to 89/90, Bob's 34 goals and promotion out of the old Third Division, alongside fierce rivals Rovers, who pipped City for the championship.

But a couple of injuries and a dip in form saw Bob leave City in January '92, after 126 games and 58 goals. A £300,000 transfer fee took him to West Brom and 'Super' Bob went on to become a legend for a whole new army of fans, scoring 37 goals in his first full season for 'The Baggies'.

In two spells with the Midlands club he made nearly 400 appearances, scoring 131 goals. He also enjoyed a Premiership swan song with Bolton before his second spell at The Hawthorns and, in 2003, had a final league season with Cheltenham Town.

All in all, Bob, who now has his own promotions company, made nearly 700 senior appearances for his league clubs, netting 237 goals – a true legend.

Bob (left) looks on as team mate Russel
Bromage (right) battles for possession.

Super Bob Taylor today.

SHAUN TAYLOR

If you asked the fans of Exeter City, Swindon Town or Bristol City to name their all-time best line-up, former centre half Shaun Taylor would probably feature in all three. Very much a fans' favourite, he's won promotion on four occasions; scooped up numerous Player of the Year awards; captained all the clubs he's played for and made over 500 senior appearances. Which is all the more remarkable, when you discover that he didn't become a professional footballer until he was 23.

Born in Plymouth, Shaun was a plumber by trade, turning out for Western League sides, before Exeter City realised they had a gem of a defender right on their own doorstep.

'Colin Appleton was the manager who took the gamble on me stepping up into full-time soccer,' recalled Shaun. It was probably the best and safest gamble that Appleton ever took, as Shaun's displays in the heart of the Grecians' defence soon endeared him to the fans. Under Appleton and later Terry Cooper, he went on to make 200 appearances for the club, leading them to promotion into the old Third Division in 1990.

'I had some great times at Exeter, but after five years wanted to prove myself in one of the higher divisions,' said Shaun. Although reluctant to sell their defensive star, Exeter couldn't afford to turn down a £200,000 cheque from Second Division Swindon and within 12 months Shaun was leading the club into the top flight.

'Glenn Hoddle took me to Swindon and I knew that working under him could only make me a better player,' he pointed out. Sadly, Hoddle moved on and although John Gorman tried valiantly to keep Swindon in the Premiership, it wasn't to be.

'We got to the Premiership on merit and although it was short lived, it was a fantastic experience,' said Shaun. 'Also, as a centre half, it was exciting to be marking the likes of Ian Wright, Alan Shearer, Mark Hughes and Peter Beardsley.'

During his five years at Swindon, Shaun won their Player of the Year on five occasions. But, with the arrival of Steve McMahon as manager, Shaun's days were numbered at The County Ground. 'I was thirty-three and he thought that my legs had gone, so I was happy to take up a new challenge when Joe Jordan paid out £50,000 to take me to Ashton Gate.'

After Jordan left the club, John Ward took over. 'John is a very nice bloke and an excellent coach, who knew what he wanted and deserves a lot of credit for getting the club promoted in 1998,' said Shaun, who skippered that promotion-winning side.

Shaun went on to make over 100 appearances for City, before he decided to call it a day in 2000. 'I'd had a few niggling injuries and felt that I couldn't perform to the standards I'd set myself, so that was that,' he admitted.

After a spell as reserve team coach at Ashton Gate, Shaun joined up with former team mate Gary Owers as assistant manager at Forest Green Rovers. 'It was the right time to move into management and I felt very disappointed when we were axed – but that's football.'

Married to Jacky, the couple live in Devon and have two teenage sons, who are both showing promise as footballers. Twice just missing out on managing Exeter City, Shaun spends much of his time scouting.

Shaun in his City days.

Shaun Taylor today.

STEVE THOMPSON

It may have been a short career at Bristol City for Steve Thompson, but he's not likely to forget his time at Ashton Gate, before he departed for a spell in the forces and then over a decade serving Yeovil Town.

A member of both the Devon and the England schoolboys team, Steve was spotted by former City star Gerry Sharpe. He joined The Robins towards the end of the Alan Dicks reign, just as the club was spiralling down the leagues and heading for bankruptcy.

'Bob Houghton gave me my full-time contract, but by that time the club was in freefall,' said Steve. After Houghton and his assistant Roy Hodgson had left, the club turned to the younger players. But a nasty illness put a temporary stop on Steve's progress. 'I went down with chicken pox, a very debilitating illness,' he explained. 'My parents thought I'd had it as a child, but obviously I hadn't. I lost a lot of ground because of that.'

But Steve did have the satisfaction of marking his debut, in the final game of the 81/82 season, with a goal. 'We were two down at Doncaster. I came on as a sub, managed to score, Ricky Chandler got an equaliser and we finished the season with an away point. Those weren't the most pleasant of times, what with the departure of the Ashton Gate Eight. All the youngsters had been thrown in, but it was just too much to expect them to cope.'

Starting life in the bottom division and with Terry Cooper doing his best to turn things around, the side literally sank to rock bottom with a resounding 7-1 hammering at Northampton. 'I think that was our lowest ebb,' said Steve, a member of the team that day. 'Northampton's old ground was a pretty depressing place at the best of times and, as you can imagine, the coach trip back was pretty grim.'

Steve went on to make 16 senior appearances for the side, but with the club literally counting every penny, he was released in January '83. 'I think I was one of sixteen they let go. I had the chance to go to Joe Royle's Oldham. Looking back I should have taken it.'

A chance to stay in the area with Torquay United seemed ideal, but it didn't work out and Steve dropped into local non-league football and then joined the Royal Air Force. 'I became a PT instructor, played a lot of football, travelled the world and got made up to corporal during my nine years in the RAF,' he said.

It was during his service days that Steve signed for Slough Town, before Wycombe (still non-league then) paid a £25,000 transfer fee for his services. Steve was to enjoy some glory days with the club, helping them to league and cup success and ultimately a place in the Football League. A spell at Woking followed, before, in 1998, he began his long association with Yeovil Town. Here he played for the club, coached, was manager on two occasions and, until his departure in February 2009, was assistant manager.

Married to Carole, the couple have three young sons and live in the Yeovil area.

A young Steve Thompson in his City days.

Happier times at Yeovil, Steve with former manager Russell Slade.
(photo: Nigel Andrews)

TONY THORPE

Born in 'Salt and Lineker country', a stone's throw from Leicester City's Walkers Stadium, it's no wonder that Tony Thorpe had such a 'crisp' finish in the box – scoring 137 league goals during a career that included being City's top scorer for three seasons.

'I was on Leicester's books as a youngster, but moved on to Luton Town when I was eighteen,' revealed Tony.

His big break came when manager Lennie Lawrence moved Tony from midfield to striker. For the next six years Tony could do no wrong, netting half a century of league goals in his first spell with the club.

Although Luton were relegated in 1996, the following year they just missed out on promotion, with Tony netting 32 goals to earn the prestigious Golden Boot Award. He also walked off with the club's Player of The Year and the Players' Player of the Year awards. 'It was just one of those seasons that all strikers dream about,' said Tony.

Understandably, his goal-scoring exploits were soon attracting offers from other clubs and in February '98 an £800,000 transfer fee took him to Fulham, but the move didn't work out.

Enter Bristol City, who had just won promotion to the First Division (now The Championship) and were convinced that Tony would get the goals needed for them to do well. Sadly, despite paying out £1million for his services, they were wrong.

With City struggling and Tony unable to reproduce his goalscoring form, loan spells at Reading and then his old club Luton followed. 'By the time I came back, John Ward had gone, but the slide continued.' The arrival of Tony Pulis as manager did nothing to improve Tony's situation and he returned to Luton for another loan spell.

'After Tony Pulis left I was called back to Ashton Gate and, under the new regime, recaptured my old form,' said Tony.

For the next three seasons Tony was City's top scorer and his final tally was 61 goals in 151 appearances. 'I loved the Ashton Gate pitch and in Brian Tinnion the club had one of the best crossers of a ball in the division.'

With his contract up at the end of the 2001/2 season, Tony exercised his right to move on, rejoining Luton Town once again. 'City fans never forgave me for leaving, but football's a short career and you have to do your best for yourself and your family.'

Tony was to spend another year with Luton, before moving down the road to rivals QPR for a knock-down £50,000. 'QPR were in the division above and this was probably my last big chance.'

After scoring 10 goals in his first season at Loftus Road, Tony was loaned out to Rotherham for a short period, before being released in the summer of 2005. A move to Swindon was not a success, before Tony moved on to Colchester United, helping the club to promotion to The Championship. Next stop was non-league Stevenage, before Tony had one last shot at league football with Grimsby. Illness in the form of gastroenteritis and then an eye problem brought his career to an end. 'I had a scan on the cornea which revealed extensive damage and I had to pack the game in.'

These days Tony makes the odd scouting trip for Leicester City. Off the pitch he has his own tiling business and lives in the Leicester area with wife Natalie and young sons Morgan and Alfie.

Tony in his playing days.

Tony Thorpe, with former QPR team mate Dennis Bailey at a recent testimonial game.

DEREK VIRGIN

A former PE and geography teacher, Derek Virgin was one of many footballers in the fifties and sixties who combined soccer with a career off the soccer pitch. 'There were quite a number of what they called 'part-time' footballers in those days,' said Derek. 'Footballers at that time weren't particularly well paid – unlike today – and it was a short lived career.'

Derek had been spotted as a teenager, by City scout Cliff Morgan, playing in the Somerset Senior League. 'I made my City debut as an amateur in December 1955 – we beat Plymouth Argyle six-nil at Ashton Gate,' he recalled.

Having completed two years National Service with the Somerset Light Infantry and three years with St Luke's Teacher Training College in Exeter, Derek arrived at Ashton Park Secondary Modern School, just a corner kick away from the City ground. He'd already had a few senior games for City as an amateur, before signing as a part-time professional and made his first appearance as a pro in a home match against Sunderland in October 1958. 'We won four-one and I was fortunate enough to get two of the goals.' And take note of the crowd that day – over 25,000. 'Another interesting fact about that game was that the crowd were entertained at half time by singer Frankie Vaughan,' added Derek.

'Looking back to those days at City, Alec Eisentrager was a big influence, as was Tommy Burden, who became a good friend. Then there was Johnny Watkins and, of course, John Atyeo, who also played as a part-timer while teaching. I told him once I was thinking of packing in teaching and going full time. Don't do it, was his response.

'There were some great characters in the game then and some very good footballers, like Tom Finney and Stanley Matthews,' continued Derek. 'I've got some great memories and can recall playing against John Charles and Jackie Charlton in the same Leeds side and also remember a young Bobby Moore marking me in a reserve game against West Ham – and I scored.'

Between 1955 and 1961, Derek was to make close on 30 senior appearances for City and, finishing as he began, scored in his last game, a 2-1 defeat at Halifax Town. Released by The Robins at the end of the 60/61 season, he was to enjoy two seasons at Bath City, where the legendary Malcolm Allison was beginning to cut his teeth in management circles. 'Malcolm was the best manager I ever played for. An excellent coach who was way ahead of his time.'

Like City goalkeeper Adriano Basso, Derek is very much a committed Christian. 'It was on 20th September 1962 that I found Jesus and it was a massive change in my life,' he said. His commitment to his faith saw Derek leave Ashton Park for Moorlands Bible College in Devon, followed by six years travelling the world to spread the Christian message. 'I went all over – Israel, France, Germany. It was tough at times, but well worth it.'

Returning home, Derek taught Religious Knowledge and PE at Homefield School in Christchurch for three years and then had over 20 years at Wadham Community School in Crewkerne, before retiring in 1994.

An Elder of the Crewkerne Christian Fellowship for 17 years, Derek and his wife Beryl have two daughters and four grandchildren.

Derek Virgin, fifties-style at City.

Time to reflect: former school teacher
and City forward Derek Virgin.

KEITH WAUGH

Fans of a certain age will remember 1973, when mighty Leeds United were beaten one-nil at Wembley by underdogs Sunderland. They will, no doubt, recall that magnificent double save by keeper Jim Montgomery to keep Leeds out, as Sunderland clung on to their lead. One year later, another goalkeeper, Keith Waugh, signed for the club and even today, is a Sunderland season-ticket holder.

'I was born in Sunderland and signed on for them after leaving school, the year after their Wembley triumph,' said Keith, who would later go on to be Bristol City's custodian for over four years. The only problem for Keith was trying to dislodge Montgomery from the number one jersey – an impossible task, as the ace shot stopper went on to complete a record 623 senior appearances for 'The Black Cats'.

Desperate for first-team action, Keith gladly accepted the opportunity to go to Third Division Peterborough United on a free transfer. 'My first game was against Brighton away. They had scored something like thirteen goals in their previous two games,' recalled Keith. 'We lost, but only one-nil, and I was pleased with my performance.'

Keith was to spend five years with 'The Posh' and was virtually an ever present for three consecutive seasons. Another Wembley hero, Sunderland goalscorer Ian Porterfield, was Sheffield United's manager and, remembering the youngster's agility between the sticks, paid £100,000 to bring him to Bramall Lane.

Over the next three seasons Keith was to enjoy two promotions with 'The Blades', moving up from the Fourth to the Second Division. But an injury put him out of the side and his understudy grabbed his chance with both hands. 'Paul [Tomlinson] came in and did very well and I couldn't get my place back, but that's football,' said Keith.

Anxious for first team action, Keith had a month on loan at Cambridge United, before signing for City (initially on loan) in December '84. 'Terry Cooper was manager and I have to say, he's one of the best I've ever played for.'

By the start of the 85/86 season, Keith had made the goalkeeper's position his own, going on to make 225 appearances for the club. Three games stand out for him. 'Going to Wembley in the Freight Rover was wonderful. We got there two years running and a lot of players never get to play there once, never mind twice.' And the other game? 'Playing Forest in the semi final of the League Cup,' answered Keith. 'Under Cloughie they were a top drawer side and we would have beaten them if Alan Walsh's shot, two minutes from normal time, had gone in instead of hitting the post.'

In the summer of 1989, with Keith out of contract, came the chance of a move to Coventry City. 'With hindsight, I should have stayed put,' he admitted. 'I only had one game in the top flight with Coventry.'

Keith moved on to Watford for three seasons, but played just a handful of games. He was also youth coach there for a while. 'I thought that it was about time I got myself a 'proper job', so I joined the police,' he said.

Having started more than 14 years ago as 'a bobby on the beat', Keith progressed to the rank of Detective Constable, worked within CID and is now with the public protection unit. He is based in Bedford, where he lives with wife Julie. They have a daughter Gemma, son Simon and three granddaughters.

Keith the keeper in action against Bristol Rovers.

Keith and his wife Julie.

KEN WIMSHURST

When Ken Wimshurst first started playing football, it was a completely different way of life. For example, there was National Service and, later, the scrapping of the maximum wage for footballers. And if there hadn't been National Service and the increase in footballers' wages, City stalwart Ken Wimshurst might never have come to Bristol.

Born in South Shields, Ken's first club was Newcastle United. 'I joined Newcastle when I was nineteen and played mostly in the reserves,' said Ken, who also had a loan spell with Fourth Division Gateshead.

By this time Ken had been 'called up' for the obligatory spell of National Service duty. 'I had left the area and was in the RAF, which led to my signing for Wolves,' recalled Ken. But while the scrapping of the maximum wage for footballers meant that they could be better rewarded, it also meant that clubs had to reduce their playing staffs to afford increased wages and Ken left without playing a first-team game.

'Luckily, I was spotted by Southampton while playing for the RAF in Hampshire and joined the club in 1961. I spent the best years of my playing career at The Dell, alongside the likes of John Sydenham, George O'Brien and Terry Paine.'

Ken was to clock up over 150 games for 'The Saints' and was a member of the promotion side that pipped Bristol City for a place in the top flight in 1966. 'I don't remember playing against City at Ashton Gate that season, but I'm sure I played in the return game.'

In October 1967, Ken became new City manager Alan Dicks' first signing, at a transfer fee of £15,000. 'Alan was the reason I signed for City. He ran the club very well and was very much a hands-on manager,' pointed out Ken.

Over the next five seasons, most of which were spent avoiding the drop back into the Third Division, Ken was to clock up 168 games for City. Originally a wing half, he moved to right back towards the end of his playing days, appearing in 29 senior games in his last season.

'While I was still playing at the age of thirty-five, I was also coaching and taking the necessary courses,' said Ken. 'When I was offered the opportunity to join the coaching staff, I decided to retire from playing.'

While on the coaching staff, Ken was to be part of the club's greatest achievement – promotion to the top flight in 1976. 'That was great for Bristol and it was fantastic to be part of it.'

Ken was to have eight years coaching at Ashton Gate, but, by 1980, City were struggling, having been relegated back to the old Second Division. Having had 13 years at the helm and masterminded the side's rise into the top flight, Alan Dicks was sacked.

Although Ken had a three-week spell as joint caretaker manager he knew it was time to go. 'Things changed after Alan left and, although I was sorry to leave Bristol City, it was time to go.'

After City, Ken enjoyed success as manager of an Egyptian team in Alexandria, taking his side to a top-six place and the cup semi-finals two years running. These days he can be found living with wife Meg on the Costa Del Sol. Between them they have four children and six grandchildren, while former City striker Ricky Chandler is a son-in-law.

It's that successful 1975/76 line up again,
with Ken on the far right of the middle row.

Ken today, enjoying life in Spain.